Wisdom Beyond the Classroom

Real World Advice to Last a Lifetime

by
Ryan Lockee

Copyright © 2020 by Ryan Lockee

All rights reserved. Printed in the United States of America. No part of this book may be used or reproduced in any manner whatsoever without written permission except in the case by brief quotations, articles and reviews.

DISCLAIMER & LIMIT OF LIABILITY: With the exception of quotation references, the names, characters, businesses, places, events, locales, and incidents are used in a fictitious manner. Any resemblance to actual persons, living or dead, or actual events is purely coincidental.

The teachings, practices, activities, techniques, examples, ideas, principles, and methods in this book, although useful, are not a replacement for the medical or psychological advice of a licensed professional. The content in this book is a general guideline and not as an analysis, antidote, diagnosis, prognosis, cure, recommendation or solution for specific ailments or problems. You should always consult with a qualified medical practitioner for assistance with any physical or psychological issues you may have.

Self-published

FIRST EDITION

ISBN: 978-1-7348184-4-4

www.wisdombeyondtheclassroom.com

Acknowlegement

I want to thank you for picking up *Wisdom Beyond the Classroom*. I've spent the last two years putting in a lot of time and energy writing and thinking about it, and I feel grateful to be able to share it with you. I've learned from many influential people, and some of their sage advice and ideas have been woven into the story with care. Their quote and name are at the back of the book, in the "Quote References" section.

I've been blessed to have a lot of amazing people in my life and am a better person because of the people I've listened to, learned from, and surrounded myself with. A big shout out to my parents, siblings, extended family, friends, teachers, students, coaches, mentors, everyone that played a part in helping this book get published, and of course my beautiful wife and son. I love you and thank you!

Dedication

Whether you're a current student or haven't been in school for years, our growth and learning is lifelong, so I dedicate this book to you. My intention is that you will not only find *Wisdom Beyond the Classroom* enjoyable, but that it will help you on your own path. A path where you have the ability to tap into your potential and inner wisdom by shaping your mind to become your greatest asset and rid yourself of limiting beliefs. May the stories, simple lessons, and words of wisdom add value to your life.

Table of Contents

Acknowlegement iii

Dedication iv

Introduction viii

Chapter 1: What's In It For Me? [Classroom] 1

Chapter 2: Expand Your Comfort Zone [Auditorium] 10

Chapter 3: OWWWs, OMMMs, and Ocean Views [Classroom] . 15

Chapter 4: You're a Visitor [Auditorium] 21

Chapter 5: Unclutter Your Mind [Classroom] 32

Chapter 6: The Change Starts with You [Auditorium] 39

Chapter 7: The Greatest Secret [Classroom] 46

Chapter 8: 1 in 400 Trillion [Auditorium] 51

Chapter 9: Everything Is Energy [Classroom] 57

Chapter 10: Impermanence, Pain, and Suffering [Auditorium] ... 63

Chapter 11: Plant and Nurture [Classroom] 74

Chapter 12: Inner and Outer Reflections [Auditorium] 84

Chapter 13: A Story That Serves [Classroom] 89

Chapter 14: Meditation [Auditorium] 94

Chapter 15: As if It's Already Happened [Classroom] 105

Chapter 16: Mindfulness and Displaying Emotional Intelligence [Auditorium] 116

Chapter 17: You Are More Than Enough [Classroom] 122

Chapter 18: Visualization [Auditorium] 129

Chapter 19: Comparing Doesn't Serve You [Classroom] 139

Chapter 20: Combining Meditation, Mindfulness, and Visualization [Auditorium] 148

Chapter 21: Your Habits Define You [Classroom] 157

Chapter 22: Take "Try" Out of Your Vocabulary [Auditorium] 170

Chapter 23: Failure Is Part of Success [Classroom] 179

Chapter 24: Follow Your Own Path [Auditorium] 187

Chapter 25: Attitude of Gratitude [Classroom] 192

Chapter 26: Practice and Share [Auditorium] 200

Chapter 27: Be Kind [Classroom] 207

Quote References 211

About the Author 217

Introduction

If you look up the definition of school, you'll find that it's defined as a place where people, especially young people, are educated. Students are taught how to read and write, along with a variety of subjects that include mathematics, science, history, geography, art, and music. While much of what we learn in school is important, we live in a world that is constantly changing. Acquiring and learning new skills and information will become more important and part of our curriculum, while other subjects, over time, will become less important or obsolete.

What remains constant is that we are human, and having a human experience has its challenges. Being comfortable in your own skin, learning how to manage and control one's self, shaping your mind to be your greatest asset, along with appreciating and loving yourself is a continual process. It requires guidance and is something that many people never fully embrace or develop.

We're imperfect, emotional beings with our own experiences, thoughts, beliefs, strengths, abilities, challenges, weaknesses, doubts, and insecurities. Shouldn't we be taught at an early age and throughout our school years how to: embrace who we are, put thought into the questions we ask ourselves and the attitude we choose, create better habits, and have more control over how we respond to how we feel? I certainly think so and believe that if we were taught more about personal development, it would make being human much easier with increased enjoyment, success and fulfillment. I also believe it would void us of many unwise decisions as well as put an end to a lot of the pain and suffering we cause to ourselves and one another.

As someone that taught various subjects and grade levels in the U.S. as well as internationally, my passion and interest has always been the development of the individual and is the inspiration for this book. Since we've all been in school, and because we all take on the roles of teacher and student in various parts of our lives, *Wisdom Beyond the Classroom* comes to you from the perspectives of a wise teacher and his students, who all teach and learn from each other.

Now, take a deep breath and slowly exhale, you're about to meet some new characters that want nothing but the best for you.

www.wisdombeyondtheclassroom.com

Chapter 1:
What's In It For Me?
[Classroom]

"Let me ask you a question, class. Have you ever had an assignment or been asked to do something, and you say to yourself, *why on earth am I being asked to do this?*" asked Mr. Ocean.

Almost everyone in the class was nodding their head or said yes.

"Or you say to yourself, *this doesn't seem very important. When am I ever going to use this in the real world?*"

A resounding "yes" was heard throughout the classroom and one of the students shouted, "All the time Mr. O!"

"That's what I thought. Guess what? I thought the same thing when I was your age, and I still think the same thing from time to time, even as an adult!"

Mr. Ocean had a passion for teaching and the body language, the facial expressions, the different tones of voice, and the energy he displayed when speaking with his students was a sight to behold. As one of the two 8th grade teachers that had been at Jefferson Middle School for several *years, he was a master at capturing and keeping the students' attention, while being able to connect with each of them in the process. He also had great success because he saw the best in his students and had a deep care and concern for their personal development. Far and wide, parents, teachers, and students all considered him a leader and role model.*

"Let me give you an answer to that question you can use and hold onto whenever this happens. This will change the way you look at things and make a positive impact on your life," said Mr. Ocean.

He paused for a moment.

"Not everything you are taught or do in life is completely relevant. This is true when you're young and in school, and it's true when you get older. What you will find extremely useful throughout your life is your attitude and the questions you ask yourself. When you're asked to do something that you don't understand, or something you find unimportant or irritating, such as a homework assignment or perhaps being asked to help out at home, here are three questions you can ask yourself."

He looked around the room, noticing that the students were listening and wanting to know more.

"Number one, what can I learn from this? Number two, how can I be completely present with what I'm doing and do it to the best of my ability? Meaning you're not distracted with something else and that you're giving your full attention to what is in front of you. And number three, what kind of attitude would serve me best right now?" asked Mr. Ocean.

"It takes just as much or more energy and effort to be upset and frustrated as it does to be grateful and enjoy what you're doing. Throughout your life, you will be asked to do things you're not jumping for joy to do, and things will happen that are annoying, but guess what—that's okay. The primary cause of unhappiness is never the situation, but thoughts about it. Be aware of the thoughts you are thinking."

He let that sink in for a moment.

"When we struggle with or are frustrated with something, that's where the lessons are, and that's when the learning takes place. Situations like this allow you to pause, take a deep breath, and ask yourself questions that benefit you. Doing this helps you take control of how you want to think, rather than the unhelpful ways you've thought in the past. If you feel what I'm talking about, let me get a *yep yep*," said Mr. Ocean.

"Yep yep," said the class.

"Good, go ahead and get out your journals to write these questions down. Here's what I want you to write down. At the top of a new page in your journal put, 'What's in It for Me?'"

He paused for a moment.

"Below your heading, write this down ... three questions to ask myself when I feel like this. Number one, what can I learn from this? Number two, how can I be completely present and do this to the best of my ability? Number three, what attitude would serve me best right now?"

He gave the students enough time to write and repeated the questions one more time for them.

"Let me ask you a question class, when you've been asked to do something you don't want to do, what kind of thoughts run through your mind?"

About half of the students raised their hands.

"Niyah," said Mr. Ocean, pointing in her direction.

"This is stupid," said Niyah.

"Yep, I've thought that. Someone else?" he said, pointing to a different student.

"This sucks!" exclaimed Kobe.

The class laughed.

"Oh, I've thought that too. And one more," said Mr. Ocean, pointing to a different student.

"I hate this," said Andre.

"Yep, that too. So, we've got, *this is stupid, this sucks,* and *I hate this*. Does that pretty much sum up what we've thought when asked to do something that doesn't make any sense to us?"

"Yes," said the class.

"What was that? I couldn't hear you."

"Yes!" yelled the class even louder.

"Oh okay, I heard you that time," said Mr. Ocean.

The students laughed.

"I'm guessing that when you have thoughts go through your mind like, *this is stupid, this sucks,* and *I hate this,* you're not at your best. And chances are, you'll likely be in a crummy mood throughout the task and maybe longer. And you're probably not going to do things to the best of your ability. Is that a fair assumption?" he asked.

"Yes," said the students.

"Did you know that you're actually smarter when you're in a positive frame of mind than if you're not? It's true, this has been studied and proven. Your brain in a positive frame of mind is more productive, can work longer, sees more possibilities, makes better decisions, and will outperform your neutral, negative, or stressed brain. Incredible! Now you just have to remember that and keep it in mind, especially when you're in a lousy mood."

Mr. Ocean continued, "What if, instead of defaulting to negative thinking when you're asked to do something you don't understand, or when something arises in life that you don't like, you ask our three new questions instead? What then? Do you think that would change things?"

Some of the students nodded their heads, and a few said yes.

"It's easy for us to automatically think a certain way when something happens that we don't agree with or like. It's as if our thoughts take over without asking for our input. Before you know it, we've gone down the rabbit hole to negative thinking, and it can take some time before we climb back out. That's why it's a good idea to instead pause, take a deep breath, and think of questions to ask yourself that benefit you. Doing so will keep you in control, rather than your thoughts and emotions running the show," said Mr. Ocean.

He took a sip of water.

"Class, let's practice this for a moment. I want you to think of a time you were asked to do something that seemed unimportant or something you thought you'd never use in the real world."

He paused for a moment.

"Okay, did you think of one? I'm sure some of you thought of a few. Now that you have your example, I want you to think of how you responded or what you thought of, and based on your mindset, how you went about doing the task."

The students all looked deep in thought.

"Now, I want you to think of being asked to do that same thing. Only this time, I want you to imagine yourself pausing, taking a deep breath, and then asking yourself our three questions. What can I learn from this? How can I be completely present and do this to the best of my ability? What attitude would serve me best right now?" said Mr. Ocean.

He paused, gave the students some time to think about this, and then continued after about thirty seconds.

"So, what did we come up with after thinking of the three questions? Were you able to see in your mind the difference between the two scenarios? Does anyone want to share?"

About one third of the students raised their hands.

"Go ahead, Luke."

"I pictured myself in both situations, and in the second one, I felt like I had a lot more energy to do what I was asked, and I did it a lot better," said Luke.

"What were you asked to do?" asked Mr. Ocean.

"To clean my room," said Luke.

The class nodded, as if they had thought of the same situation.

"So, you had more energy, and as a matter of fact, you cleaned your room better in the second scenario."

"Yeah, and I learned something from this. I always thought it was stupid that my mom asked me to do this, 'cause it's my room and I should be able to have it any way I want. But then I thought, what can I learn from this, and a light bulb went off. My mom wants me to clean my room 'cause she's teaching me how to pick up after myself, which will be good for me when I do get in the real world. And the quicker I clean my room, the quicker I can do things I want to do, like play basketball or video games," said Luke.

"Amazing answer Luke, that's exactly why we're doing this. Let's hear from one more student," said Mr. Ocean.

This time, even more students raised their hands.

"Yes, Colleen."

"When I pictured myself the first time and then the second time, I noticed that I enjoyed what I was doing a lot more the second time around. When I asked myself, what attitude would serve me best, I pictured myself smiling and then doing what I was asked to do, and it wasn't as frustrating," said Colleen.

"What was it that you were asked to do?" asked Mr. Ocean.

Blushing, Colleen hesitantly said, "A writing assignment you gave us."

You will have two Wisdom Beyond the Classroom *questions at the end of each chapter. The first question will be about your thoughts and essential takeaways from the chapter. The second question will often be two-fold, asking specific questions about the chapter. To make sure you are fully engaged and get the most out of what you're reading, it's recommended that you answer the questions before moving onto the next chapter.*

What are your thoughts and most important takeaways from the chapter?

Think of a time when you've been asked to do something you didn't understand or agree with, or thought was a waste of time. What kind of thoughts did you immediately think, and how would the outcome of the situation have been different if you had paused, taken a deep breath, and asked yourself the three questions instead?

Chapter 2:
Expand Your Comfort Zone
[Auditorium]

As a rule of thumb, all great things start as a simple thought that's put in motion with belief and action, and this was no exception. Just a few years earlier, Viv, Leon, and Mick had a desire to give their fellow schoolmates guidance on how to live their best lives possible, and now they found themselves in new territory. They were on the stage of an auditorium, in a high school that wasn't theirs, about to speak to over 1,000 students they didn't know.

This speaking engagement wouldn't just be another tedious assembly the high school students had to attend. They were about to be schooled on topics that had the potential to be life-changing if applied. Although this was the largest audience the three students had ever been in front of, they were confident that things would go well, just as they had in the past. Speaking in front of so many people would be terrifying for most students and adults, but the three friends had dedicated many hours to working on the craft of public speaking. While some had their doubts about whether or not Viv, Leon, and Mick could make an impact on others, the three students believed in what they were doing, and in their ability to share what they referred to as "wisdom beyond the classroom"—essential knowledge to be applied in the real world that wasn't usually taught in school or even at home.

Each of the three students played an essential role in their speaking engagement, but it was the one standing in the middle that would primarily be running the show. The one in the middle, a teenage monk known as Mindful Mick, reflected in awe at how far life had brought him at such a young age. Abandoned as a baby and raised in uncommon circumstances before being adopted, he had already faced and overcome many challenges. Now he was embarking on a new adventure thousands of miles from where he started.

Standing on the stage, Mick smiled to himself as he thought of his favorite quote, "You get in life what you have the courage to ask for." He had first heard the quote a few years earlier in his homeroom at the time from his favorite teacher. That teacher, Mr. Ocean, had talked about how this only happened by aligning thoughts, beliefs, feelings, and actions, which was no small task. While it was never Mick's intention to speak in front of so many people, he knew in his heart that he had asked for this in a roundabout way. Mick had a desire to make the world a better place by connecting with and adding value to others, and helping others see the best in themselves. As if he were back in the classroom, he could hear Mr. Ocean saying, "You don't need to know the how, you just need to know the why." Mick had his why, and the how was now right in front of him.

"Yo Mick, you alright? You look deep in thought, and we're about to start," said Leon.

Mick said nothing and didn't move.

After his brief reflection, Mick took a deep breath, straightened up, raised his head, and turned his attention back to the audience. As he looked out at the crowd of people, his thoughts were of love, kindness, and compassion. Mick pictured the audience receiving these thoughts and felt connected with everyone in attendance.

Far from your typical 11th grader, Mick was confident, focused, selfless, and grateful that he and his two friends had this opportunity. Mick took the hands of his two friends and huddled the three of them together. Looking in the eyes of Viv and Leon, he spoke.

"Looking back on when we first started speaking to other students, we've come a long way. We have continued to step out of and expand our comfort zone. And what has happened because of that?"

"Well, we keep growing and learning, we help out others, and we've made a lot of friends," said Viv.

"And we keep facing new challenges that we're able to take on. I think our delivery is getting much better and we're getting more confident," said Leon.

"Yes. When we expand our comfort zone, growth and learning takes place, we lift ourselves and others up, we grow in belief and confidence, new friends are made, and the universe continually supports us," said Mick.

"Yeah, it's as if we have invisible help and guidance, and the only thing we can do if we keep going is succeed," said Viv.

"You were not meant to play small and be ordinary; extraordinary is your birthright. We have the opportunity to share insights and wisdom and help open each person up to their potential and greatness. Remember that and remember to enjoy yourself and this moment. We're fortunate to be here," said Mick.

"You're right about that; we'd be in math class right now," said Viv.

With that, the three friends huddled even closer until their heads were touching.

"Desire," said Mick.

"Believe," said Leon.

"Action," said Viv.

Then the three friends got back in their places and faced the audience. Mick stood in the middle, Leon stood to his left, and Viv stood to his right. All three took a deep breath at the same time and slowly exhaled. They were ready.

What are your thoughts and most important takeaways from the chapter?

What have you done lately to expand your comfort zone?

Chapter 3:

OWWWs, OMMMs, and Ocean Views
[Classroom]

After everyone in the class had stopped laughing at what Colleen had said, including Mr. Ocean, they continued.

"Fantastic answer, Colleen. I'm glad you were able to have much more joy the second time around with something boring I asked you to do," said Mr. Ocean.

The students laughed.

"How about a hand for those excellent examples we got from Luke and Colleen."

The class broke out into applause, and both Luke and Colleen smiled.

"Alright class, now that you have your journals out, I know you're ready for your weekly dose of 'Ocean's Why Wisdom Wednesday'! And what is the shortened version of that?" asked Mr. Ocean.

"OWWW," said the class loudly together.

"That's right, OWWW, but it doesn't hurt if you know it and apply it! And we also work on our Openness, Mindfulness, Meditation, and Mastery throughout the week, and we call that what, class?"

"OMMM," said the class loudly together.

"That's right, OMMM, like *home* without the *h*."

Mr. Ocean would incorporate several activities to make sure his students understood and enjoyed learning, and were able to stay engaged, focused, and think outside the box. Every Wednesday, Mr. Ocean fit in time to teach information that was considered outside of the curriculum but would be useful in and out of the classroom. Viv, Leon, and Mick had been in his 8th-grade homeroom a few years earlier, which is what prompted them to teach other students some of the wisdom they had gained in his class.

On the side of the classroom was a big bulletin board, with the area divided into three sections. The first section was titled "Classroom Jobs," the second section had a picture of everyone in the class and was titled, "We Are Family," and the third section was titled "OWWW," for "Ocean's Why Wisdom Wednesday." This section had a quote or saying for most Wednesdays of the year, and almost every week, a new OWWW was uncovered. The quotes were covered with construction paper that had Velcro attached to it, making it easy to reveal the new quote each Wednesday. Once a quote was shown and discussed, it remained on the board so the class could see it for the rest of the year. There were already many wise quotes[*] that had been revealed and discussed, some of which included:

---

[*] *All quotations used throughout this book are real quotes from real people. Authors' credits may be found at the back of the book in the* Quote References *section.*

You get in life what you have the courage to ask for.

Faith is taking the first step, even when you don't see the whole staircase.

There was never a winner that wasn't a beginner.

The ability to observe without evaluating is the highest form of intelligence.

You are a direct result of the thoughts you think, the people you spend time with, and the books you read.

The person who fails to plan, plans to fail.

Desire backed by faith knows no such word as impossible.

"Let me ask you a question, class. What does it mean to you to have ocean views?"

About half the students raised their hands.

"Let's hear from Tony," said Mr. Ocean as he pointed in his direction.

"If you have ocean views, it probably means you're living like a baller!" exclaimed Tony.

The students laughed or nodded in agreement.

"You're living like a baller 'cause you probably have a sweet house with ocean views, and that ain't cheap," said Tony.

"Very good point Tony. Someone else?"

Once again, about half the students raised their hands.

"Yes, Jocelyn," said Mr. Ocean.

"I think it means that you're living a pretty nice life and that you feel at peace. At least when you have the ocean views, you feel this way. And I think Tony's right; it's probably expensive if you have a house with ocean views, but I don't think it's that way for everyone. Maybe some people can have ocean views pretty easily without having to pay for the view," said Jocelyn.

"Wow, excellent points, thank you, Jocelyn. We'll take one more response."

This time about a quarter of the students raised their hands.

"Grace, go ahead."

"I was thinking of it a little differently, but I still think it goes along with what Tony and Jocelyn said. I was thinking of it more like your view or outlook on life. If you have a great view of life, then you have ocean views. If you don't have a good outlook on life, then you don't have ocean views," said Grace.

The class looked shocked at what Grace had said, and one of the students was raising his hand as if he would die if Mr. Ocean didn't call on him.

"What a fantastic answer Grace, thank you for sharing. Let's quickly hear from Justin before he falls out of his chair," Mr. Ocean said, making the class laugh.

"I got it! Ocean views are *Ocean's Why Wisdom Wednesday*! We're not just talking about having a view of the ocean, we're talking about the way we see things. That's why we have a new OWWW quote every week. Ocean views brought to you by Mr. Ocean!" exclaimed Justin.

A collective "ahhh" was heard throughout the class.

"Outstanding! From Tony's answer to Jocelyn's to Grace's and Justin's, we couldn't have scripted that any better. You nailed it! Give yourselves a hand!" Mr. Ocean proclaimed.

What are your thoughts and most important takeaways from the chapter?

Which one of the OWWW quotes speaks to you, and what are your thoughts in regard to your own "ocean views"?

Chapter 4:
You're a Visitor
[Auditorium]

Standing stage left, Leon looked out at the large audience, took a step forward, and began.

"Greetings, fellow Earthlings. I don't know if you can tell by looking at me, but like you, I'm just a visitor on this planet. I have come in human form; they call me Leon, and while I'm not exactly sure why or how long I'll be here, one thing is for sure, I plan on making the most of my time here on Earth," said Leon.

Standing stage right, Viv took a step forward and started in.

"Thanks for letting us know you're a visitor and not an alien, Leon. I'm also a visitor on this planet. The name's Vivian, but everyone just calls me Viv for short," said Viv with a big smile.

"Before we go any further," Viv continued, "I want to set the record straight for the audience. You're about to listen to a talk given for kids, by kids. I mean, it's also for teachers, and adults will benefit from the information we're about to share, but you get my point. Almost everyone here is a student, and so are we. That means this is intended to be educational and nothing short of life-changing, but also a lot of fun. So, I want you to think of today's assembly as an adventure you're about to have. You'll pick up pieces of wisdom and learn lessons. There will be funny moments, serious moments, shocking moments, and all kinds of things, just like a great adventure. Are you ready?"

Some of the students in the audience said yes, others nodded their heads, and some didn't move or say anything.

"You guys, Viv just told you that this assembly isn't gonna suck, it's gonna *ROCK*, and we're about to go on an adventure! Let's try that again. Are you ready to go on a great adventure!?" exclaimed Leon.

This time the audience came to life a little more, and a resounding "yes" was heard throughout the auditorium.

"Great job audience, that was much better, and thanks, Leon. As you were saying, you plan on making the most of your time here as a visitor on this planet. But what does that mean to you exactly?" asked Viv.

"You know, making a name for myself, getting way out of my comfort zone, and pushing the boundaries of what's possible. When it's all said and done, I plan on having my name written in the history books," said Leon.

"Sounds great, but I think the only history book your name has a chance to be written in is your own Social Studies book," said Viv.

Ignoring Viv, Leon continued.

"I plan on doing things like breaking the home-run record in the big leagues, riding 30-foot waves, and starring in my own comedy series. I'm sure I'll think of a few others, but that's a pretty good start," said Leon.

"Wow, someone thinks highly of himself," Viv teased.

"If I don't, then who will?" asked Leon.

"Good point," said Viv.

Leon shrugged.

"Honestly, I'm not that ambitious. Winning the lottery and kickin' it sounds pretty good to me," said Viv.

"That's all you want to do, win the lottery and kick it? You're selling yourself short, Viv," said Leon.

"Maybe we should poll the audience. Who in here thinks that winning the lottery and relaxing with your millions sounds like a pretty good idea?" asked Viv, as she looked out over the crowd.

This got some cheers and applause, and some of the audience members raised their hands.

"See," said Viv.

"Of course people are going to cheer about money and doing whatever you want—I mean, c'mon, that's pretty amazing. But if you actually won the lottery, don't you think doing nothing constructive with your winnings would be pretty selfish?" asked Leon.

"Whatever. Your time here on Earth doesn't sound very altruistic to me," said Viv.

Leon stared at her but said nothing.

"*Altruistic*. It means you have a concern for the well-being of others," said Viv.

"I know what it means, Viv. And I do have a concern for others," said Leon as he straightened up and looked a little more proper.

"Oh?" asked Viv.

"I do, and I probably owe a lot of it to our favorite former teacher, Mr. Ocean. And some to Mick, and some to my parents. Remember the quote in Mr. O's class?" asked Leon.

"Which one? There were a lot of them," said Viv.

"The one about giving," said Leon.

"'The secret to living is giving.' That one?" asked Viv.

"No, that was a good one, but it's the other one. 'We make a living by what we get, but we make a life by what we give.' That's the one I like," said Leon.

"Yeah, I like that one too. So, what are you trying to tell us? You're not just some surfer jock, you've actually thought this out, and you plan on giving back?" asked Viv.

"Absolutely. A man can only have so many millions," said Leon.

"Did you say man?" asked Viv.

Ignoring the comment, Leon carried on.

"Just like how we raised money in class for water wells and filtration systems in developing countries, there's a lot of good I'm gonna do. And it'll happen while I'm here as a visitor and make a difference even when I'm long gone," said Leon.

"I'm not sure how realistic all of your goals are, but I'm impressed that you want to give back to others," said Viv.

With his head down the entire time this conversation had been going on, Mick stood in between Leon and Viv. He took a step forward to be in line with his two friends and faced the audience.

"Look who decided to join us. I wondered how long you were gonna stand back there," said Leon, as he patted Mick on the back.

With his hands pressed together in the center of his chest, Mick closed his eyes, bowed slightly, and said, "Namaste." Then he opened his eyes and lowered his arms back down to his sides.

Looking out at the crowd, Leon said, "Yep, that's how he rolls. And you ain't seen nothin' yet from Master Boy Yoda."

This got a few laughs.

"Hey, that's no way to talk about Mick," said Viv.

"It's nothing. Mick and I are tight; that's just how we talk to each other. Besides, it's a compliment," said Leon.

"Anyway, *namaste* is a way of saying hello or thank you with respect and appreciation," said Viv.

"It's also a way of saying that I recognize you in body and soul and that our hearts are connected," said Mick.

"Yeah, that too," said Viv.

"My name is Mick, but many of my friends call me Mindful Mick. While I live and go to school here in this great country, I was born and raised in India, under very unusual circumstances, raised by monks. Like my two friends, I'm also a visitor on this planet and plan on making the most of my time here," said Mick.

"I'm guessing how you make the most of your time will be a little different than Leon's," said Viv.

"Yes, I'm not much of a surfer," said Mick, smiling.

The audience laughed.

"We realize that you're being spoken to by three students you don't know. We are not from a school out of state, we are not homeschooled, and we are not part of a traveling circus," said Mick.

He paused for a moment.

"We're from ... " said Mick.

"Wait for it," said Leon.

"We're from your rival school, Central High," said Mick.

Boos were heard throughout the audience.

"And they were so nice just a few seconds ago," said Viv.

"We understand. If you had the choice between throwing tomatoes and roses, you wouldn't choose the roses. But that's okay, we love tomatoes, and the three of us come in peace," said Leon as he made Spock's Vulcan "salute" hand gesture from Star Trek.

"Yeah, we get it. It's like, what could you possibly learn from three 11th graders from the archenemy, that sucky school, Central

High, right? Well, we've got a secret for you, actually quite a few of them," said Viv.

The three students paused for a moment.

"The secret is ... we are a lot more similar than we are different. While we do go to different schools and may have different opinions or ways of living, you and I and everyone here is a human being, with thoughts and feelings, hopes and dreams, fears and imperfections. We're alive at the same time in the history of humanity, on the same planet, on the same continent, in the same state, and the same city," said Mick.

"That's pretty awesome when you stop to think about it. Like, the only thing that separates us is something made up, or an imaginary line that says you go to Lincoln and we go to Central, based on where we live in the city," said Leon.

"Hmmm, kind of like our imaginary state and country lines, telling us that we can or can't do something based on where we live," said Viv.

"And it's because of these imaginary lines that we tend to stereotype, or make separations between us and them, good and bad, right and wrong," said Leon.

"That's crazy. Have you ever stopped to think about the fact that many of the people who will become your friends or family members live on the other side of one of these imaginary lines that divide people?" asked Viv.

"Yeah, and these imaginary lines are often places we think of as the rival or enemy, like a different school, town, state, or country, or someone with a different perspective than our own," said Leon.

"Looking at it from a larger perspective, with an open mind, there's something called the 'Overview Effect.' Many astronauts have reported that, once they viewed the Earth from space, they never looked at their own personal or national perspectives and interests the same way again. They viewed life and everything on our planet as one, without divisions and human-made borders," said Mick.

"Wow, talk about seeing things from a much larger perspective," said Viv.

"Yes, exactly. The fact is, we are so much more similar than we are different, and while we're here as visitors on this planet, it's important that we love one another, that we help out, accept, and appreciate each other the best we can. With a united mentality instead of a divided one," said Mick.

"Yeah, even though we go to different schools, we think of you as friends we haven't met yet," said Leon.

"Nice, Leon, I like that," said Viv.

"Leon, Viv, and I are appreciative of your time and will make sure that what you learn today is valuable, enjoyable, and something you can use in your own life. Today we are here to talk to you about things that aren't typically spoken about in school. We're here to discuss wisdom that will benefit you beyond the classroom. We will be sharing information to help you create and be in control of your own amazing and unique life," said Mick.

"Yeah, with more certainty and less stress," said Viv.

"As much as we love technology and the ability it gives us to communicate with others, it's fair to say that it can also distract us from being able to focus on what's in front of us and be completely present. I ask that if you have your phone out or something else that might be distracting you, please put it away now, and make sure the sound is off," said Mick.

"And I'll do the same, right after I get a selfie of us on stage," said Leon.

The three friends moved closer to each other, turned so their backs were facing the audience and struck a goofy pose. "Say cheese, everybody!" called Leon, and the audience responded loudly. Leon took the picture and the three friends turned back around to face the audience.

After putting his phone away, Leon said, "As mentioned, we're here to share valuable information with you, and guess what—this information has nothing to do with your school subjects."

This got a few cheers from the crowd.

"If you were a visitor or a guest somewhere that you knew was not forever, what kind of visitor or guest would you want to be? Would you be a visitor that does enough to get by, that doesn't contribute much, and is then soon forgotten after you leave? Or one that leaves a mark, making the world a better place than you found it, and lives an incredible life?" asked Mick.

He paused and everyone was silent.

"Obviously, Mick, leaving this place better than we found it and living an incredible life sounds much better. As visitors on this planet, it's important that we do our part and take care of this place," said Leon.

"Yeah, and it doesn't seem to be happening. Not only is there a ton of changes happening in the environment, but the amount of waste we produce in our country alone is astonishing," said Viv.

"It is! I read the other day that just in the U.S., we use more than 38 billion plastic water bottles every year," said Leon.

"Every year? And did you say *billion* with a *B*? Holy—" said Viv, before being cut off by Leon.

"Yeah, with a B. Crazy, right? And apparently, most of the bottles don't even end up getting recycled. On top of that, 10% of the plastic we use each year ends up in our oceans," said Leon.

"What? Do you guys hear this? We gotta do something about this!" proclaimed Viv as she looked out at the audience.

Audience members could be seen nodding in agreement.

"Which leads us to the next thing we want to speak on. That is, *the change starts with you*. The thoughts you think, how you respond to your feelings, the way you view yourself, others, and the world around you, and the actions you take. It all starts with you," said Mick.

What are your thoughts and most important takeaways from the chapter?

With the time you have here as a visitor on our planet, what are some of the things that are most important for you to do?

Chapter 5:
Unclutter Your Mind
[Classroom]

When the clapping for the answers given about ocean views stopped, Mr. Ocean continued.

"Before we reveal this week's OWWW quote, I want everyone to take a nice deep breath in through their nose and hold the breath for a moment," Mr. Ocean said.

He paused briefly, then continued.

"Now go ahead and release the breath and say *ahhh*."

"Ahhh," said the class.

"Feels good, doesn't it? Okay, one more time. Take a deep breath in through your nose and hold the breath for a moment. And release."

"Ahhh," said the class.

"It's good to know we can always come back to the breath to center ourselves and relax. Now, let me ask you a question that might seem odd but has relevance. What's something that you do to clean yourself?" asked Mr. Ocean.

The question seemed to perplex some students, while about half of the students raised their hands.

Mr. Ocean pointed and said, "Yes, Laura."

"Take a shower," said Laura.

"Yes, that's true. What else?"

More hands went up, and he called on another student.

"We also wash our hands and brush our teeth," said Katie.

"Yes, and hopefully, all of you do these things every day. Otherwise, you suffer for it, and so do other people," said Mr. Ocean as he held his nose and waved his hand in front of his face.

The students laughed.

"When your house is dirty, what happens?" he asked.

Half the hands in the class went up.

"Yes, Brad," said Mr. Ocean.

"Well, if my house gets dirty and doesn't get cleaned right away, my mom goes crazy. She says she feels like her life is out of control if the house isn't clean, so we help her out as much as possible. Or we tell Dad to call the cleaners," said Brad.

"Helping Mom pick up or calling the cleaners so she doesn't go crazy. Good answer, Brad. Let's hear from somebody else."

Again, about half of the students raised their hand.

"Yes, Jamar."

"Our house stays pretty clean because my sister and I have chores to do, and we take turns cleaning the house. You know, things like picking up, doing the dishes, and taking out the trash," said Jamar.

"So, you and your sister help keep the house orderly and clean. That's good to hear, Jamar," said Mr. Ocean.

He paused for a moment.

"What I hear from your answers is that picking up the house and keeping it clean is something that needs to be done. Otherwise things get messy and cluttered and people might go crazy."

The students smiled and nodded.

"So, how does this apply to both our OWWWs and OMMMs?" he asked.

Blank stares from the class.

"Let me rephrase the question. How does the act of cleaning, something we are applying in our OWWWs, also apply to our OMMMs? Think about it. How can the cleaning impact the M's in OMMMs?"

As if a few light bulbs went on, some hands started to go up.

"Yes, Jie," said Mr. Ocean.

"*Mindful* is one of our M's. If you're mindful about how keeping your house, or your room, or your desk clean makes you feel, you will do a good job of keeping these places clean because you feel better when they're clean," said Jie.

"Excellent answer, Jie. What else, class?"

Six hands went up.

"Yes, Alyona."

"*Mastery* is another of our Ms. If we wanted to keep things clean and did that every day, we would become masters of cleaning," said Alyona.

"Masters of cleaning, that has a nice ring to it. Good answer, Alyona. What else class?" asked Mr. Ocean.

Three hands went up.

"Yes, Corinna."

"You guys, I think we're missing the main point and what Mr. O is trying to tell us. Think about it. We meditate in here, like, every day. It's one of our M's in OMMM, and we're talking about cleaning. Why do you think we meditate? Because it helps us clean out our minds of any garbage we're putting in it," said Corinna.

As if the entire class understood all at once, they let out a collective "Ohhhh."

"No, not OHHH, you mean *OMMM*," said Mr. Ocean.

The class laughed.

"Bravo Corinna, you got it! Yes, meditation is healthy in a lot of ways, and that's why we do it, 'like every day.' Just by sitting in silence for even a few minutes each day, concentrating on your breathing, and coming back to your breathing when you notice your mind wander, you are uncluttering your mind and what goes in it.

It's the same reason we take mindfulness breaks throughout the day."

Mr. Ocean paused for a moment.

"Think about it. If it is important to clean your house or your room or your desk so that it wasn't cluttered, why wouldn't you do that every day for something that's even more important to keep clean? Meditation does that for your mind so that you can start fresh, with an uncluttered mind. An uncluttered, open mind that is quiet, positive, healthy, and strong, with the kind of thoughts in it that you choose."

He paused again for a moment, then continued.

"If someone were to give you a piece of trash or something gross to hold, chances are good that you wouldn't take it. The same should be true for your thoughts and what you choose to believe and put in your mind. Other people's opinions and our own thoughts come and go, and you have the choice to discard that which is of no benefit to listen to or hold onto. The same is true when it comes to forgiving yourself and others. Forgiveness is a wonderful gift you can give to yourself, which allows you to unclutter your mind and let go of that which doesn't serve you," said Mr. Ocean.

"That's brilliant! Oh, sorry for blurting out," said Liliana.

"No problem, Liliana, I'm glad it makes sense to you. Class, like a guard dog protecting a house, stand guard at the gate of your mind, letting in only what benefits you, and keep the garbage out. Remember, your mind is your greatest asset, so be careful what you put into it."

Now, before continuing and revealing our OWWW quote, put your pencils *down*, stand up, and shake your bodies out!" Mr. Ocean directed.

This particular phrase was the cue for students to stand up and move their bodies. Sometimes Mr. Ocean played music with the "shake your body break," and sometimes he didn't. Either way, it would usually last 30 to 60 seconds. Not only did the students love this break, but it was also healthy for their bodies and brains; it reenergized them and got them to refocus when they sat back down. This one lasted for 45 seconds, and all of the students welcomed the break.

What are your thoughts and most important takeaways from the chapter?

It's important to unclutter your mind, spending some quiet time alone each day with yourself. What do you need to let go of that's cluttering your mind and not serving you, and what do you need to change if you're not already giving yourself the gift of some daily quiet time?

Chapter 6:

The Change Starts with You
[Auditorium]

"That was a nice transition, Mick. And it sounds like that quote by Gandhi that says, 'Be the change you wish to see in the world,'" said Viv.

"Precisely. The change you wish to see in the world starts with you," said Mick.

"Like the way we think, act, speak, and treat ourselves and others, right?" asked Leon.

"Yes, and some of the topics we'll be covering like meditation, visualization, and mindfulness will contribute to this," said Mick.

"Wow, we're covering all those topics today? It's like an Ocean's crash course all in one sitting. And let me tell ya, Ocean views will change your reality," said Leon.

"He's referring to our amazing former teacher, Mr. Ocean, who taught us many things that, dare I say, most teachers on the planet don't teach," said Viv.

"Meditation, visualization, and mindfulness will be like a hot dose of wisdom, confidence, and clarity for everyone here," said Leon.

"Before we go any further, I think it's best if we get these people moving around a bit," said Viv.

"Agreed," said Leon.

"What do you think? Do you want to move around and shake what your momma gave ya?" asked Viv as she pointed to the crowd.

The question got a mixed reaction from the audience.

"I don't know about you, but if I'm sitting and listening to someone for more than ten or fifteen minutes without feeling engaged in what I'm learning, or if I'm not able to move around, I get antsy and start to lose my focus, especially if it doesn't include using my phone, computer, or television," said Viv.

"For sure. Sitting quietly and listening to someone without the use of technology is healthy, but it isn't the easiest thing to do," said Leon.

"Exactly. So, throughout our informative, exciting, and fascinating presentation that you're enjoying immensely and will learn a lot from, we're gonna keep you people moving. Anytime you hear me say, 'shake what your momma gave ya,' that's your cue to stand up and dance," said Viv.

"And don't worry, you won't be dancing without music—that would be awkward for everyone, including us," Viv continued.

This got a few laughs.

"We'll have music playing as soon as you hear the cue," said Leon.

"Are you ready for your first one?" asked Viv. "I think you are! Let's give it a test run. Alright, everyone, go ahead and stand up and shake what your momma gave ya!" she exclaimed.

The music started in and most of the audience stood up, but only about a quarter of the audience was moving. The music faded after 15 seconds, and the audience started to sit back down.

"For your first attempt, I'm gonna give you two and a half stars out of five for your effort. Not terrible, but I know you can do much better," said Viv.

"Yeah, whether you've got some dance moves or not, no one cares what you look like, just have fun with it," said Leon as he started doing The Robot.

"We're gonna have you do this again, and this time I know you're gonna get up and really go for it. Now, on the cue, I want you to get up and out-dance the people standing to your right and left. You ready?" asked Viv.

She paused for a moment.

"Alright, stand up and shake what your momma gave ya!" yelled Viv.

The music came back on, and this time everyone stood up, and nearly two thirds of the audience began dancing or moving their bodies. After thirty seconds, the music faded, and the audience sat back down.

"Yeah, that was much better! We'll be doing that from time to time, so if you didn't give it all you had this time, another opportunity is yet to come," said Viv.

"Alright, let's get back to what we were talking about," said Leon.

"The change starts with you. Not anyone else, just you. Have you ever asked yourself the question, who do I want to be today?" asked Mick.

"Huh? Who do I want to be today? I don't get it," said Viv.

"When I ask that question, *who do I want to be today*, or *who do I get to be today*, I'm referring to asking yourself questions that put intention into what direction you want to give yourself. To be the kind of person that also asks yourself questions like, *how do I want to interact with others, how can I make a difference,* and *how can I be excellent in what I'm doing*? When you do this, you become the kind of person that intentionally thinks, feels, and acts in a way that aligns with who you want to be, for yourself and with others," said Mick.

"So, you're referring to asking yourself questions about being more thoughtful about what you want," said Leon.

"Precisely," said Mick. "And whatever it is that you want to see in the world, remember that it first starts with *you*. In the way you treat yourself, the questions you ask, and the intentions you have. When you do these kinds of things, you grow on a personal level. You also have more self-control, more creativity and imagination, and you also take care of what is happening outside of you to the best of your ability. This includes how productive you are, what you contribute, how you connect with others, and the energy you put out into the world. These play an important role in our overall well-being, confidence, and in the direction our lives take."

"So, let me get this straight. We just shared that the change we wish to see in the world, in others, and ourselves starts with us, and in the questions that we ask ourselves. We're also going to be sharing other life lessons that aren't typically taught in school. This gained information is actually life changing and will lead to better, happier, and more fulfilled lives for everyone that uses it. Correct?" asked Viv.

"Correct," said Mick.

"That's what I thought. This information is priceless. So why on earth are we giving this information away for free? That sounds like a cash cow for us—we should have charged an entry fee!" proclaimed Viv.

Leon gave Viv a look as if to say he agreed and gave her a thumbs-up.

"The information we're sharing is not ours to keep and it wasn't ours to begin with. These universal truths can be used in the real world and have been around as long as humans could think, feel, and understand how powerful thoughts are, including the direct connection between thought and reality. We're just putting it in a new way that is easy for people to understand," said Mick.

"That makes sense, but I do love me some money and can always use more of it!" exclaimed Viv.

"Our pay for offering this information will reap much more than monetary compensation. Our reward is that we will directly help change the planet for the better, one person at a time," said Mick.

"Well, we better start doing some serious recruiting; that's gonna take some time," said Viv.

"What do you think we're doing here?" said Leon.

"Every day throughout our world, love, kindness, compassion, thoughtfulness, and healing is taking place. But so is pain and suffering, hatred, violence, intolerance, cruelty, and thoughtlessness. With all the misguided misery taking place, it's up to each one of us to change the direction our world is headed. Even the smallest gesture matters, like a ripple in a pond, to influence, impact, and make big changes. It first has to start with you, on an individual, personal level," said Mick.

"Yeah, that makes sense. How far do you think this ripple could go?" asked Viv.

"Your changes can and will cause a ripple, positively affecting those around you, including friends, family, and classmates. And as a school, we have the ability to impact our community positively, and so it goes. Our community can and will influence our city. Our city will influence our county, and then, our state. Our state impacts our country, and our country impacts our continent. In turn, our continent will impact our planet, our planet will impact our solar system, and yes, our solar system can even impact our galaxy," said Mick.

"That's far out!" exclaimed Leon

What are your thoughts and most important takeaways from the chapter?

What kind of questions are you asking yourself, and what kind of things are you doing to be the change you wish to see in the world?

Chapter 7:

The Greatest Secret
[Classroom]

After the "shake your body" break was done and the students were back in their seats, Mr. Ocean continued.

"This week's OWWW is very important. In fact, it is one of the most important of all. Are you ready for it or should we put it off until next week?"

"No!" shouted the class.

"Alright, without further ado, drumroll please," said Mr. Ocean.

All the students in the class started drumming on their desks.

"Here you go!" Mr. Ocean pulled off the orange-colored construction paper, which made the sound of Velcro ripping apart and revealing the new quote:

The greatest secret is that you become what you think about.

"You've heard a lot of secrets in your life, but I just revealed the greatest secret of them all—that you become what you think about! You are now in possession of something very special that many adults don't even know about. Whether you like it or not, you create your life. Your dominant thoughts shape your life. Now, let's say it all together class."

"The greatest secret is that you become what you think about," said the class.

"Take a moment and write that down in your journal," said Mr. Ocean.

He waited patiently while the students wrote in their journals.

"The greatest secret just revealed is what we're talking about when we speak of uncluttering our minds, having thoughts that serve us, and a belief in ourselves. What's more important, what someone else thinks about you, or what you think about yourself?"

"What you think," said the students.

"Yes, what you think. There's a saying that goes, 'Everyone is a genius, but if you judge a fish by its ability to climb a tree, it will live its whole life believing that it is stupid,'" said Mr. Ocean.

The students laughed.

"But do we do this? Do we have a tendency to sometimes believe what others think about us, more than what we think about ourselves?" he asked.

"Yes," said the students.

"What other people believe about us can have an impact, and our words can be used to empower or disempower ourselves and others. But what other people believe is not what's important. What's important is what you believe about yourself. You *become* what you think about; it's the greatest of all secrets. Now that you know the secret, how is it going to serve you moving forward throughout this adventure we call life? What are you going to do with this information?" asked Mr. Ocean.

He paused for a moment, allowing the class to think about what was asked, then continued.

"How many of you believe that you're a leader?"

The students looked around the room at each other. Five students raised their hands with confidence, while six more reluctantly raised their hands.

"So, we have a room of 30 students, but only 11 of you raised your hand? I don't think you're giving yourself enough credit, or that you've given it enough thought ... Here are some questions for you to answer rhetorically. Do you believe and think that you're creative? That you're a genius? That you have unlimited potential and are destined for greatness? Do you think that you can accomplish anything you put your mind to?" asked Mr. Ocean.

He paused for a moment as the class thought about his questions.

"Look at our quote again. *The greatest secret is that you become what you think about.* Some of you may or may not believe and think that you're cut out to be a leader. Or that you're creative, a genius, destined for greatness, or that you can accomplish anything you want. My response to that would be that you don't have to believe your negative thoughts, and you weren't born knowing how to tie your shoes, walk, or talk either, right?" asked Mr. Ocean.

The students smiled and nodded in agreement.

"If the greatest secret is that you become what you think about, what kind of thoughts are you putting in your head about yourself? Are you loving and kind towards yourself? Have you been telling yourself positive things that build your confidence, like what you can accomplish, how valuable you are, what you're capable of, and how strong and intelligent you are? Or have you been telling yourself negative things that don't serve you and put limits on what you can accomplish?"

"Spend time contemplating who you want to be. The mere process of contemplating who you want to be, begins to change your brain."

What are your thoughts and most important takeaways from the chapter?

Now that you know the greatest secret, what are you going to do with it?

Chapter 8:

1 in 400 Trillion
[Auditorium]

"It's important to be aware of and understand how unique you and everyone else is and to appreciate that. To help you create your amazing life, it makes sense to talk about how special you are," said Mick.

"Yeah, some of us are really special and unique," said Viv in a dramatic tone.

Viv's comment drew some laughter.

"I knew that I was unique at an early age, but it wasn't for reasons you might think. Growing up and being raised by monks in India is very special and unique in its own right, although doing so did not pave an easy road for me, socially speaking. Especially if you take my feet into account," said Mick.

"Your feet? What, do they stink?" asked Leon.

Leon's comment made the audience chuckle.

"Growing up as a monk, my outfit consisted of a robe and sandals. This sometimes made it difficult to make new friends that weren't monks, especially when people noticed that I have ... six toes on each foot," said Mick.

"What?" exclaimed Viv and Leon at the same time.

"I know what you're thinking; what are the odds of that happening? Well, it's more common than you might think, with thousands of babies born each year with what is known as *polydactyly*," said Mick.

"Poly-dac-ta-lee?" asked Viv.

"Yes, having more than five fingers or toes on one, or each hand and foot. I have this on both feet, and while I'm fine with my very unique trait, that wasn't always the case," said Mick with a slight grin on his face.

The audience looked shocked, and some started to laugh.

"Whoa, like the six-fingered man on *The Princess Bride*," said Leon.

"I love that movie!" shouted Viv.

"As you might imagine, having such a unique trait is not easy for a kid. When I first discovered that I was different than other kids, I was very self-conscious and never wanted to take off my socks," said Mick.

"Yeah, I wouldn't either, and I certainly wouldn't be shouting it from the rooftops that I have extra toes. I can't believe you just spilled the beans about that to everyone here," said Leon.

The audience laughed.

"We are all unique, and no one is perfect. Not you or me or anyone. What I've discovered is that having this rare trait has been more of a blessing than anything," said Mick.

"Yeah, how so?" asked Leon.

"I've learned to embrace and accept myself for who I am, and to take what others say about me with a grain of salt," said Mick.

"Grain of salt?" asked Viv.

"Yes, to not take things personally. To not care so much about what others think or say, especially when it's negative or meant to be hurtful," said Mick.

"Well, that's good, and you're right, no one's perfect, but I think these people want to see if what you're saying is true," said Leon as he looked down at Mick's feet.

"I know you can't see them because I'm dressed in normal clothes with socks and shoes on, but they're down there. While some think it's funny or weird, I believe it makes me more exceptional, balanced and grounded. I also believe that we are all vulnerable when it comes to something about ourselves, and that we need to embrace and have the courage to accept and express who we are," said Mick.

Viv and Leon gave each other a look as if to say, 'he makes a good point.'

"Being human means that we're not perfect. It's easy for us to focus on what it is about ourselves that we don't like and to shame ourselves for it. How we're not good enough, or loving enough, or smart enough, or not good looking enough, or not creative enough, or whatever it is that we feel like we're lacking," said Mick.

"Yeah, I do that. My self-talk is good at times, and then other times I'm quick to beat myself up about silly things such as the way I look or the way I talk, or about the way I reacted to someone. Then I tend to overcompensate around others by being loud and acting like I've got it all figured out when, in fact, I'm not happy with myself about something," said Viv.

"Thanks for the honesty, Viv. That must be pretty hard, you know, the not being perfect thing," said Leon. He paused long enough for her expression to go blank.

"I'm just kidding, Viv. I do the same thing, except that I'm quieter than usual, hoping someone doesn't point out or notice that I made a mistake or that I'm not having my best day. I can be pretty hard on myself as well," said Leon.

"Thank you both for your honesty. Doing these things is very common. In fact, it makes you human. None of us is perfect and yet we are made perfectly with our imperfections. Do you know what the odds are of being born just the way you are?" asked Mick.

He paused, and both Viv and Leon shrugged.

"The odds of being born just the way you are ... is close to 1 in 400 trillion," said Mick.

"No way! Seriously? That's cray cray!" exclaimed Viv.

"Wow! That *is* crazy, like winning the most outrageous lottery ever. But how do you come up with such a large number? It sounds absurd," said Leon.

"Yes, the number is so large it's hard to comprehend. Based on the chances that your parents met, and had you specifically, and that you came from a whole lineage of ancestors that had children down the line, make you 1 in 400 trillion. You can find a breakdown of the numbers online," said Mick.

"I think I need to write that down and put it somewhere so I can see it every day. Kind of like a reminder about what a precious gift life is," said Viv.

"That's an excellent idea, Viv. It is a miracle that we are here. You and I, and everyone that you know, is a miracle. And let me ask you, are you living your life with gratitude? Are you living each day like the gift and blessing it is?" asked Mick.

Mick paused for a moment, and the audience was silent.

"Sometimes," said Viv.

"I do, but not all the time. It's easy to take for granted," said Leon.

"And are you treating yourself and others like 1 in 400 trillion, like the miracle that each one of us is, embracing yourself and others in a kind and loving way? Or are you focused on other's imperfections, on your imperfections, and the negative things in your life?" asked Mick.

Once again, the audience fell silent.

What are your thoughts and most important takeaways from the chapter?

Your life is a miracle and a blessing, and so is the life of everyone else. If your thoughts, beliefs, feelings, words or actions don't reflect this, what change(s) could you make?

Chapter 9:

Everything Is Energy
[Classroom]

The following Wednesday in Mr. Ocean's homeroom, the class continued OWWW time.

"Alright class, it's that time of the week again. Are you ready?"

"OWWW," said the class.

"Good, me too. And this week we get a bonus. Our OWWW will come in the form of two quotes. Drumroll please," said Mr. Ocean.

The students immediately started drumming on their desks. As they did, Mr. Ocean turned off the lights and flipped a switch, which projected his computer screen on the whiteboard.

"Take a look at the quote from Albert Einstein that appears before you. I'll read it aloud."

Everything is energy and that's all there is to it. Match the frequency of the reality you want, and you cannot help but get that reality. It can be no other way. This is not philosophy. This is physics.

Mr. Ocean read the quote to the class, then paused for a moment. A hand went up.

"Yes, Brent," Mr. Ocean said.

"Mr. O, I don't get it. I mean, I get the fact that you become what you think about, but what does it mean that everything is energy?" asked Brent.

"That's a great question, Brent. Let me answer it this way. Have you ever been around someone and their energy is so incredible, so positive, that it's like you can feel that energy and it makes you feel good?"

"Oh yeah," said Brent.

"Or in the opposite way, have you ever been around someone and their energy is so negative that you can also feel it, and it makes you want to get away from them as fast as you can?" asked Mr. Ocean.

"Definitely," said Brent.

"And have you ever been minding your own business, not paying attention to what's going on around you, perhaps you're reading something or looking at your phone, when all of a sudden you feel someone's eyes on you? Sure enough, you look up, and someone is looking at you."

"Yeah, that has happened to me," said Brent.

"That's happened to me too," said another student.

"Exactly. These are examples of energy being given off. You and I and everything in our universe is made up of energy. Now, let me ask you another question. Does it take energy to do something, like say, build something with your hands?" asked Mr. Ocean.

"Yes, it does," said Brent.

"And does it require energy to think about something when you're trying to come up with an answer?"

"Yes," said Brent.

"So, if you have a thought, which is energy, you can turn it into reality by matching the frequency of what you want. For example, an architect can have an idea, a thought of what he or she wants to create. Then they can write or draw what's known as a blueprint of that idea, and with the feeling and belief that their blueprint can become a reality, they can design it until it's exactly what they want in its physical form. Does that make sense?"

"Yes, it does, thanks," said Brent.

"Great, thank you for the question," said Mr. Ocean.

He paused for a moment and scrolled down on his computer screen, which revealed another quote.

"Here's our second quote, it comes from Nikola Tesla."

If you want to find the secrets of the universe, think in terms of energy, frequency, and vibration.

"This quote is along the same lines with the Einstein quote. If the name Tesla sounds familiar to you, and you're thinking of the cars, that's correct. The company Tesla was, in fact, named after Nikola Tesla, who is long dead, but was an engineer and inventor.

His contributions to the design of the modern alternating current electricity supply system are still used today," said Mr. Ocean.

He paused briefly.

"Class, you are, in fact, the architect of your own life. Regardless of your outside circumstances, you can choose to live with great energy on the inside, which can include living with things like humor, joy, love, gratitude, and abundance. That energy then creates a vibration, and that vibration of energy puts out a frequency that the universe matches and sends back your way. It's as if you're able to set your energetic speaker to a certain vibration and get back exactly what you want. Hence the term, you get what you give. Does that make sense?"

Almost everyone in the class either nodded or said yes, and one student raised his hand.

"Yes, Ethan," said Mr. Ocean.

"Mr. O, this is a cool concept, and I just had an idea that goes along exactly with all of this. These quotes about energy, frequency, and vibration—this is just like changing the radio station. When I get in my mom's or dad's car, I change the settings of the radio until I get the station I want. We can do the same thing in our life, simply by sending out the right kind of energy," said Ethan.

"That's a fantastic analogy, Ethan. And to take that a step further, what happens when the radio frequency isn't coming in exactly how you want?"

"Well, I change the station until there's no static, and then the music or whatever I'm listening to is clear," said Ethan.

"Exactly. And this is what happens in our reality. Sometimes things come back to us the way we want, and sometimes they don't. When they don't, it's like the universe is telling us that we need to make big or little changes to get what we want, like getting the right frequency back on the radio. It's not that the universe is punishing us; it's just responding to the vibrational energy or attitude that we're giving off," said Mr. Ocean.

He paused to let this sink in, and the students looked at their teacher as if they were just told the most profound thing they had ever heard.

"Thank you for the great question, Brent, and thank you for the clever example with the radio, Ethan."

"You're welcome," said Brent and Ethan at the same time.

"Incredible, isn't it, class? You become what you think about, and your thoughts become things because everything is energy. Whatever the mind can conceive and believe, it can achieve. To make something a reality, you've got to think about what you want with focus, believe that it can happen with feeling, and put in the work to make it so. Feeling is emotion, emotion is energy, and energy is magnetic," said Mr. Ocean with a dramatic use of his hands and fluctuation in his voice.

The students laughed and smiled.

"Go ahead and write down the Einstein and Tesla quotes that are on the board. Along with those quotes write down the words, Chinese Bamboo Tree, which I'll explain soon."

What are your thoughts and most important takeaways from the chapter?

To match the reality of what you want, are there small or big changes you need to make in the energy you're giving off? What are some of those changes?

Chapter 10:

Impermanence, Pain, and Suffering
[Auditorium]

"Yesterday's history, tomorrow's a mystery, today is a gift, and that's why it is called the present," said Mick.

"Did you just make that up? That's awesome! Wait, I think I heard that on Kung Fu Panda," said Viv.

"Ha! Yeah that's amazing and goes perfectly with the 1 in 400 trillion," said Leon.

"We need to do our best to keep that in mind every day, because as much of a blessing life is, our lives are painful at times and will not last forever. And let's face it, life can be hard, people are not always nice, and kids can be mean. The notion that sticks and stones will break our bones, but words will never hurt, doesn't seem to be very accurate. Words can hurt," said Mick.

"Life's a gift, and oh, by the way, it's full of pain, people often suck, and you're going to die. Way to build us up, and then have us come crashing down," said Leon.

The audience laughed and Mick smiled.

"Unfortunately, there are many forms of pain, or what some refer to as suffering. Pain and suffering occur every day for young people as well as adults. Among other things, this includes abuse, stress, violence, addiction, depression, bullying, and suicide," said Mick.

"Well, that's true. All you have to do is turn on the TV. It's like negative, depressing news has become the norm," said Leon.

"This is not something we can ignore. We have to deal with these problems head-on, for ourselves and others. If these forms of pain, like the ones just mentioned, are happening to you or someone you know, it is imperative that you reach out and get or give help," said Mick.

"Yeah, and the sooner, the better," said Viv.

"We, as humans, don't have complete control over experiencing pain—it's inevitable. It will happen. But suffering, on the other hand, is a choice," said Mick.

"Wow, that sounds profound, but what exactly does that mean?" asked Leon.

"It means that painful things in our life will happen. We can't change that. But when we wallow in our pain and stay there longer than we should instead of moving away from it, then we are causing ourselves suffering. In this case, the suffering is a choice; we are choosing to stay there," said Mick.

"Like when we get fixated on something negative?" asked Viv.

"Yes, such as reliving a painful experience over and over again; we are causing ourselves unwanted suffering. Doing this is not something we have to do, and yet we tend to do it anyway. The thoughts in your mind, what you focus on, and the way you treat yourself has a lot to do with how much suffering you allow yourself to experience. This is why we talk about self-worth, and another reason we'll be discussing meditation, visualization, and mindfulness," said Mick.

He paused for a moment.

"While life can be difficult and painful at times, it's also important to keep in mind that we live in a world of impermanence," said Mick.

"Impermanence?" asked Leon.

"It means that nothing lasts forever, including our lives. It is not permanent. It is impermanent. And whether it's fast or slow, everything constantly changes," said Mick.

"Everything?" asked Viv.

"Change can occur slowly. It can also occur quickly. But it is always happening," said Mick.

"How about an example?" asked Viv.

"Alright, take popularity, for instance. While it's unimportant to some, it is very relevant in school and important to many students. Regardless of its importance, and whether or not it is happening slowly or quickly, it does change; it is impermanent," said Mick.

"Doesn't seem to change much for me," said Viv as she flipped her hair back, looking confident.

"Oh yeah, what about that time when all your girlfriends were mad at you because—" said Leon.

"Okay, moving on, everything is impermanent, as you were saying, Mick," Viv interjected.

Viv's comment got a few laughs from the audience.

"Someone may or may not be popular in their class or grade, or outside of school, but circumstances and people change. A change in popularity could happen in several ways. Someone could move, change their environment, get a new job, form different ideas and beliefs, develop new relationships, or change social circles. Whether or not popularity is important to you, it is impermanent," said Mick.

"That's probably refreshing for a lot of people to hear because it can also cause a lot of pain, and probably suffering," said Leon.

"Indeed. If we are experiencing pain or suffering, it will not last forever. There are preventative steps that can be taken to move you or someone you know away from the various forms we've mentioned," said Mick.

"How?" asked Viv.

"For starters, having patience. Are you patient enough with yourself and your circumstances? Time itself is a healer, and we often need to be more patient. Though I understand this can be difficult to comprehend, especially if one's pain has turned into stress and suffering, and is all-consuming and constantly on the mind," said Mick.

"Yeah, it's like if you're suffering or worried about something, it's hard to focus on anything else," said Viv.

"It also helps to ask yourself the right questions," said Mick.

"Like what?" asked Leon.

"If you are suffering or stressed about something, or don't like something happening in your life, here's a few questions that should bring you answers. The first question, and maybe the most important is, *what is it that I'm focusing on? Is it on things I want, that bring me joy? Or am I focusing on things I don't want that cause more suffering?* This is why most people suffer; they continue to focus on the wrong things instead of the right ones," said Mick.

"Yep, that makes total sense, and something I've done many times," said Viv.

"Other questions include: H*ave I taken the necessary steps to move away from suffering or something negative in my life? Or do I continue to do the same thing? What kind of language do I speak to myself internally? Is it kind and loving, or do I put myself down? Do I forgive myself and others so that I may heal, or do I hold onto grudges, which only causes more suffering? Am I taking care of my physical body, and do I carry myself well? Overall, do I treat myself lovingly and kindly, and do I believe in myself? Do the people I hang out with treat me well and believe in me? What kind of things am I reading and spending my time doing? Have I reached out for help if I need to?*" said Mick.

He paused for a moment.

"If you're not happy with the answers you get when you ask yourself the right kind of questions, it's time to start making some changes," said Mick.

"Well, that makes sense, and those are great questions, but what if you don't know where to start? What if you feel like you're making an effort to make changes but you're still having a hard time—like you're stuck. Then what?" asked Viv.

"You may need to work a little harder, take things one step and one day at a time, recognize that you are making progress, and celebrate your small wins. Often, we need to be a little more patient and kinder towards ourselves. If it's something serious, such as being bullied, going through something very difficult, having extremely unhealthy thoughts, or feeling depressed, you may need to reach out to someone that cares, someone that can help," said Mick.

"Yeah, I speak from personal experience when I say that the times I've felt depressed or have gone through something difficult and I don't share what's going on, it's even worse. In the hardest times, it's really important to reach out and get help," said Leon.

"That's for sure. And you mentioned bullying, Mick. Just like popularity, I know that bullying is impermanent, but it sure sucks. And I know it happens every day, that others mentally, physically, and verbally abuse kids and even adults. How do we stop that from happening?" asked Viv.

"Since it does happen every day, with over a thousand kids in this auditorium, it's probably affected everyone in here to some degree. I'm guessing you've been the victim of a bully in the past or present, or you know someone that is experiencing bullying right now," said Mick.

"Or you're the one doing the bullying," said Viv.

"Yeah, and if that's happening, *not cool!* We hope that the information you're getting today will help if you are being bullied, give you a voice if you see it happening to someone else, or move you away from being that kind of person if you're the one doing the bullying," said Leon.

"Because it is extremely prevalent in our schools today, let's talk about bullying for a moment. Bullying comes in all forms, which include physical, verbal, social, and cyberbullying. The first thing to understand is that, if someone is being bullied, it most likely has very little to do with the person that is the victim and almost everything to do with what is happening internally for the bully," said Mick.

"Really, how so?" asked Viv.

"What is going on inside a person usually shows itself on the outside. That means your thoughts and feelings tend to present themselves outwardly, through your words and actions. If someone is happy on the inside and at peace with themselves, what are the chances that they're going to be mean and bully others?" asked Mick.

"Very unlikely," said Viv.

"People that bully others tend to have self-esteem issues, a need to fit in or be liked by others or are hurting internally. Whether it's their self-image, insecurities, or something going on in their life, they're usually not happy and are manifesting that outwardly by trying to hurt others. These are not powerful, strong people like they would have others believe. They're people who are hurting and crying out for help by inflicting pain on others," said Mick.

"Wow, I never thought of it like that," said Viv.

"If someone is bullying others, they most likely have been bullied by someone else and will be abusive towards another they deem as an easy target to make themselves feel better. This is not to make an excuse for the bully; it's for people to understand that a bully is probably not equipped or resourceful in knowing how to get help with their difficulties," said Mick.

"Yeah, clearly not," said Viv.

"As Leon mentioned, the tools we give you today will help you with stress or internal suffering that you feel. People need to be shown compassion if they are the victim of bullying, and as hard as it may be, bullies need people to show them compassion as well," said Mick.

"Being compassionate to someone that's a jerk? You know that's asking for a lot, right? Compassion is important, but so is standing up for yourself," said Leon.

"Standing up for one's self is important, and so is understanding that we're all human, even the person doing the bullying. We all experience pain, we have all experienced suffering, and we all deserve to get help when help is needed," said Mick.

"Ok, that makes sense. Then what? Someone has this information, now what do they do?" asked Viv.

"To the best of their ability, someone targeted by a bully should not give the bully power over them. That's what the bully wants. Instead, they should either ignore what is happening, stand up for themselves, have a conversation with the bully, or take appropriate action by getting help from someone that can stop the bullying from happening," said Mick.

"You mean be a snitch?" asked Leon.

"Getting help is sometimes what is best for pain and suffering to stop, no matter if we're talking about bullying or something else. In regard to bullying, getting help is often necessary for the victim of bullying. It's often necessary for bullies as well. The bully will eventually have to face their inappropriate behavior, which in many cases, involves asking for help. Asking for help is not cowardly; in fact, it takes great courage," said Mick.

"What happens if the person doing the bullying is more than one person, or is an adult, such as someone with power or even someone close to you, like a family member?" asked Viv.

"The same applies. No one should be treating others poorly, certainly not an authoritative figure or a relative. That doesn't make it any more justifiable," said Mick.

"For sure," said Leon.

"When it comes to dealing with pleasant and unpleasant things in life, who do you want to be? Do you want to be someone that gives your attention and energy to things that are unpleasant and painful, causing prolonged suffering for you and those around you? Or do you want to focus on the positive and on solutions?" asked Mick.

He paused and the audience was silent.

"The same thing applies when you hold grudges or when you don't forgive others. When you do that, you end up holding onto negative energy. *You* end up suffering, not the person that caused you pain. Learning to forgive others is not just about compassion and forgiveness; it's about releasing negative energy and feeling the way you want to feel. Forgiveness allows us to heal and let go of the past," said Mick.

"Wow, those are great points," said Leon.

"Pain is a fact of life, but not something to fear. Rather, you should recognize that when pain occurs, it will not last forever. If you take appropriate action, your pain will not turn into prolonged, unwanted suffering. What we focus on expands, so put your attention on what it is that you want, not on what you don't want," said Mick.

"Another great point," said Viv.

"And when it comes to impermanence, it is a fact of life. Nothing lasts forever, which is all the more reason to be grateful for what you have and make the most of each day," said Mick.

"I like that, and I think everyone here gets the point we're making about pain, suffering, and impermanence," said Leon.

"Yeah, I agree, nothing lasts forever, and it's time to end the pain and suffering for anyone that needs to move around. Are you guys ready? Well, ready or not, it's time for everyone to get outta your seats and shake what your momma gave ya!" shouted Viv.

The music came on, and the audience rose to their feet.

What are your thoughts and most important takeaways from the chapter?

Understanding the notion that everything is impermanent, what can you look at differently in your life? Knowing the difference between pain and suffering, what is something you could do to prevent or stop suffering, and if you or someone you know is the victim of bullying, what is a good solution to stop what is happening?

Chapter 11:
Plant and Nurture
[Classroom]

When the students finished writing down the Tesla and Einstein quotes and the words, Chinese Bamboo Tree, Mr. Ocean continued.

"Thoughts become things, and we're able to focus our energy and match the frequency of the reality we wish to see. Whatever the mind can conceive and believe, it can achieve. What a concept! That means you can become a success in anything you choose. I want you to think about this for a moment. How would you define the word success?" asked Mr. Ocean.

After giving the students about ten seconds to think, he asked for a volunteer to answer the question.

"Yes, Keisha."

"I think that success is accomplishing something you set out to do," said Keisha.

"I completely agree. Success can be defined as the progressive realization of a worthy ideal. In other words, you have to take consistent action towards the attainment of your goal. If you're interested, you will do what is convenient; if you're committed, you'll do whatever it takes. Do you see the difference? You have to do something over and over consistently, knowing that you are making progress, even when there seems like there's little to no progress being made. Class, have you ever heard about the Chinese Bamboo Tree?" asked Mr. Ocean.

A few of the students said "no," while others shook their heads.

"The Chinese Bamboo Tree is just like other plants and trees. It requires proper nutrients like fertile soil, water, and sunshine. But what's unique about it is that the tree will develop a solid and deep foundation of roots underground, long before any growth is seen above ground. Would someone like to guess how long it takes until the tree shows signs of growth?"

Over half of the students raised their hands.

"Yes, Katie?" said Mr. Ocean.

"Four months," said Katie.

"No, longer than that. I see your hand was up, Luke. What's your guess?"

"One year," said Luke.

"No, even longer than that. I see your hand was also up, Leo. What do you think?"

"I think it's probably close to a year and a half," said Leo.

"That would be a long time to have to wait to see any progress, but it's much longer," said Mr. Ocean.

The students looked surprised by this.

"Believe it or not, the Chinese Bamboo Tree won't show any sign of growth until it's been growing for five years."

"No way!" cried Alyona.

"That's impossible!" shouted Jake.

"Are you making this up?" asked Laura.

Chuckling, Mr. Ocean said, "I am not making this up. On top of that, in its fifth year, when the tree finally starts to grow, it will grow 80 feet in just six weeks!"

"What?!" exclaimed the students.

"That's insane!" hollered Andre.

"I agree, it's quite remarkable. Talk about delayed gratification! Could you imagine waiting five years for something before you saw any progress?" he asked.

Some of the students said "no," and others shook their heads.

"The Chinese Bamboo Tree is very similar to many things you will pursue in your life. Difficult challenges and extraordinary accomplishments will require you to put in the time needed to develop a solid foundation before you will start to see results. It will also require a strong, burning desire to accomplish your goals, a belief in yourself and your pursuit, along with consistent action and dedication."

"Don't forget patience," said Paulo.

"Yes, and patience. And you have to be able to persevere in doing these things, even when it looks like very little or no progress has been made. Otherwise, doubt will creep in, or you will start to believe other people's opinions that you can't accomplish what you set out to do," said Mr. Ocean.

He paused for a moment.

"Is there something you want to obtain and will work hard at getting no matter what, even when others doubt you?"

Some of the students nodded their heads yes, while others just looked at him, contemplating the question.

"When you believe something about yourself and know what you want to achieve, some people will believe in you, and others will doubt you. Regardless of what others think, you have to stay firm in what you believe about yourself. Remember, you are made up of energy, and can direct that energy to create what you want," said Mr. Ocean.

He paused again briefly, then continued.

"Let me ask you a question, class. With the proper nutrients, even after a few years, does the Chinese Bamboo Tree give up on growing?"

"No," said the students.

"You're right. It doesn't. It will plant roots as deep as it can and when it starts to grow, it will grow as big and as tall as it can. It doesn't stop because it feels like stopping, or because other trees might judge it."

"Does a baby give up on walking?" he asked.

The question got a funny reaction from the class. Some of the students shook their heads while others smiled at the notion of a baby giving up on walking.

"No. But could you imagine if a baby *did* give up on walking based on what other people said? 'Oh, little Mikey tries hard and is so cute, but he just keeps falling. I don't think he'll ever learn to walk,'" said Mr. Ocean in a funny voice.

The class laughed.

"If that was something baby Mikey heard enough times until he believed it, he might stop trying to walk. And if that was happening all over the planet, then what? We'd have half of the population crawling around on all fours!" he proclaimed.

The class laughed again, this time even louder.

"Can you imagine seeing adults crawling around, just because they didn't believe they could walk?" asked Mr. Ocean, trying not to laugh along with the class.

"Letting other people's opinions limit what we can do happens all the time, doesn't it, class? So, what's the difference between a tree, a baby, and those of us that let doubt take over?"

About a third of the hands went up in the class, and Mr. Ocean pointed at one of the students.

"A tree and a baby don't let anything stop them from getting what they want," said Aaron.

"Exactly, Aaron. A tree naturally wants to grow to its fullest potential, and a baby naturally wants to crawl, walk, and run. They aren't interested in someone else's opinion about whether they can or cannot do these things. But as we get older, we often change our own beliefs about ourselves and what we can accomplish based on our doubts and what other people think. It's as if we let our doubts run the show, or let someone else's opinion be more important than our own. Who has an example of this happening in your own life, or in the life of someone you know?"

A few hands went up in the class.

"Kobe," said Mr. Ocean.

"I think my mom doesn't believe she's a good cook," said Kobe.

"Why not?"

"Because she's heard my dad say that more than once," said Kobe.

"Your mother cooks food for the family, and your father has complained about the cooking often enough that your mother doesn't believe she's a good cook. Is that what I'm hearing?" Mr. Ocean asked.

"Yes," said Kobe.

"Oh, well, that is a shame. Class, do you think Kobe's mother would be a better cook if she were more confident in her cooking abilities, rather than listening to anyone else?"

"Yes," said the class.

"And do you think there's a pretty good chance that Kobe's mom once believed and told herself she was a good cook?"

"Yes," said the students.

"So the seed was probably planted that she was a good cook, but negative opinions eventually made her believe otherwise. Just because a seed is planted, and we believe we can accomplish something does not necessarily mean it's going to happen. The seed has to be planted on fertile ground, and it has to be nourished with water and sunshine consistently. It helps to get encouragement from others, but most importantly, you have to relentlessly believe in yourself no matter what others say. You have to be in control of what you believe, tell yourself, and take action. You have to do these things consistently to see the results you're looking for," said Mr. Ocean.

He paused for a moment.

"Class, do you know what the word *empower* means?" he asked.

A few students raised their hands.

"Yes, Kristy."

"I think it has something to do with giving power," said Kristy.

"Yes, that's correct. Empowering yourself or others is like giving power, confidence, or strength to something. When you believe something and speak that which you believe, you have the ability to empower. That means that the words you speak to yourself and others are powerful."

He paused for a moment, then continued.

"While we've revealed that the greatest secret is that you become what you think about, what we think and then speak into our lives is extremely important. Studies have shown that something is ten times more powerful if you say something out loud, rather than just think about it. You can change your world by changing your words. That also works in the opposite way where our negative talk is even more powerful than the positive words we speak, so be mindful of what you say."

He paused again briefly.

"Kobe, you can be the one to empower by planting a seed of confidence for your mother, in her belief and ability to be a better cook. The next time your mother makes a meal, thank her and let her know that you think the meal was delicious, and that she's a good cook. Continue to do that, and she'll eventually believe it herself."

Kobe's eyes lit up.

"After a while, your mother's meals will probably start tasting better, and she might even get more adventurous and creative in her cooking. And I bet that your father will eventually change his mind as well," said Mr. Ocean.

"Thank you, Mr. O," said Kobe.

"You're very welcome."

"Just like the Chinese Bamboo Tree, if you desire, believe, and take action on something you want to accomplish, chances are good that it will take time before you see significant results. Patience will serve you well. And just as you would plant a seed on fertile ground and nurture it with water and sunshine, you must plant the idea of what you want in your mind with confidence. Then you must consistently cultivate that idea with positive thoughts and take the actions needed to achieve your goal. In doing so you use the law of energy and are able to match the frequency of the reality you wish to see."

Mr. Ocean waited for a few moments, letting his words sink in.

"Now, put your pencils *down*, stand up, and shake your bodies out!" he directed.

What are your thoughts and most important takeaways from the chapter?

Are the seeds you let yourself or others plant in your mind benefiting you? What can you do to nurture your thoughts consistently, and take action on what you want?

Chapter 12:
Inner and Outer Reflections
[Auditorium]

As the music slowly faded, everyone sat back down.

"In discussing pain and impermanence, we can't choose to avoid them. They're facts of life. But we do have a choice when it comes to suffering, and in choosing how we think and who we want to be. The next part of choosing who you want to be is about reflections," said Mick.

"Reflections? Like from a mirror?" asked Viv.

"Yes, sort of. I'm talking about reflections of your inner and outer world, which directly correlates with what we've already discussed, that the change starts with you," said Mick.

"What do you mean?" asked Viv.

"Let's use public speaking as an example of this. Most people, including my past self, have built up public speaking as something scary or terrifying. If this is the way someone feels on the inside, it will most likely be obvious, based on their actions on the outside," said Mick.

"Yeah, you can usually tell when someone is nervous about speaking, kind of like how I felt the first time we spoke in front of a bunch of students," said Viv.

"The same is often the case in the words we speak, the actions we take, and the emotions we express. Through these expressions, we show what is happening on the inside of us. When you take the time to do things internally for yourself, like reflection and meditation, you tap into your own inner wisdom and set yourself up for external success. The healthier and happier you are on the inside, the more it will reflect on the outside," said Mick.

"In other words, your success or struggles happening outside of you are usually a mirror image for what's happening inside of you. Is that what I'm hearing you say?" asked Viv.

"That's exactly what I'm saying. Everything is created twice, first in your mind and then in reality. Your outer world is a reflection of your inner world," said Mick.

"That makes total sense. What I find is, the better I feel, the more it shows on the outside, just like a mirror. If I'm feeling good about myself and confident, that's reflected, and others take notice. If I smile at someone, people tend to smile back, even strangers," said Leon.

"Yeah, and the same applies when we're not feeling good, and not acting as friendly as we could be. If we behave like a jerk, others will likely act like a jerk in return," said Viv.

"Yes, you get back what you put out. If you want things to go a certain way outside of yourself, first you have to work on things from the inside. If you want to have more, you have to give more.

If you want more love, for example, show more love towards yourself and others. If you want more respect and appreciation, first you have to think it, feel it and believe it for yourself, and also give it to others. You can have whatever you want and can create an amazing life, but first, it must start within yourself, with your thoughts and feelings. Then, it will reflect outside of you," said Mick.

"I'm in complete agreement with this, but what happens when you feel good on the inside and things aren't going the way you want outside of you?" asked Viv.

"In the midst of movement and chaos, keep stillness inside you. We live in a world that is constantly changing and things will happen that are not to your liking. Regardless, you still get to choose what you think about, focus and reflect on," said Mick.

"That makes total sense. I think everyone understands the fact that our outer world is a reflection of our inner world. Right, audience? Are you getting this?" asked Leon.

There were a few random things shouted, but the word "yes" could be heard throughout the crowd of students.

"I heard a lot of you say 'yes', and I think I even heard someone say, 'My reflection is beautiful.' Yeah, *you go, girl!*" proclaimed Viv.

The audience laughed.

"Using our example of public speaking again, when you've done the internal work, when you've changed your perspective and have the right attitude about it, you will realize that public speaking is nothing more than having a conversation from the heart on something you're passionate about. It's an opportunity to connect with others and something that anyone can become good at as well as enjoy," said Mick.

"Did you hear that? You're only a few terrifying speeches and hours of internal work away from being a professional speaker," said Viv.

"Now that we've talked about inner and outer reflections, whaddya say we start talking about meditation and get into the actual health benefits of it?" said Leon.

"I agree, and we also never talked about inner wisdom yet. You mentioned that just a little bit ago. How is that a part of all of this?" asked Viv.

"The health benefits you receive from meditation is a long list and will help you tap into your potential and inner wisdom, which is what makes you unique. Meditation has become increasingly popular, and there are breakthroughs in discovery happening all the time. Discoveries that show mental, physical, and emotional benefits to consistent meditation. Before we get into the many benefits, let's define meditation first," said Mick.

What are your thoughts and most important takeaways from the chapter?

How can you use the knowledge about your inner and outer reflections to your advantage, and what is it that you'd like to have or see more of in both?

Chapter 13:

A Story That Serves
[Classroom]

The following Wednesday in Mr. Ocean's homeroom, the class continued OWWW time.

"It's that time again. Are you ready for your new quote?" asked Mr. Ocean.

"OWWW," said the class.

"Fantastic, let me get a drumroll, please."

The students started rapidly tapping on their desk as Mr. Ocean pulled off the construction paper, revealing the new quote.

The story you tell yourself matters. If your story doesn't serve you, change it to one that does.

"The story you tell yourself matters. If your story doesn't serve you, change it to one that does. Go ahead and say it with me, class," said Mr. Ocean.

"The story you tell yourself matters. If your story doesn't serve you, change it to one that does," said the class.

"When we talk about the story you tell yourself, we're talking about a lot of different stories you tell yourself, about a lot of different things. It could include what you tell yourself about things that have happened in your life, where you come from, what you look like, how you view your relationships, what your strengths or weaknesses are, what someone thinks about you, something you want to accomplish, or how you feel about the future. And those are just a few examples," said Mr. Ocean.

He paused for a moment.

"Here's something for you to think about that goes along with this week's quote, class. *'Our lives are most affected by the way we think things are, not the way they are.'* Two people could have the same experience yet see it in completely different ways. Let me give you an example of that."

"There's a story of two climbers that were in great shape with similar experience and skill levels. These two climbers were ascending a very tall mountain together. At the end of a long and grueling day of climbing, they stopped to rest for the day. One of the climbers, who was mentally and physically exhausted and uncertain in his abilities to get to the top, looked up at how much farther they had to climb. This reinforced the doubts and fear he had about not being able to finish the climb," said Mr. Ocean.

He paused for a moment.

"The other climber, who was also physically exhausted but pleased with the progress they had made, looked back at how far they had come. This reinforced the fact that he was confident and certain they would make it to the top. What happened with the two climbers? What was different?"

A few hands went up and Mr. Ocean pointed to one of the students.

"One looked up, and one looked back," said Maja.

"Yes, and what else? Grace."

"They also thought differently. One was thinking positively, and one was thinking negatively," said Grace.

"Exactly. The biggest difference between the two climbers was their attitude, and the story they tell themselves. They were climbing the same mountain, yet because their thinking was so different, they were having completely different experiences. One tells himself a serving story and one tells himself a dis-serving story. This makes all the difference in the world. The climber with the dis-serving story is focused on the difficulty of the climb, the fatigue he's feeling, and how much farther they have to go in order to reach the top. The climber's brain is filled with fear, negativity, and uncertainty, which causes him suffering and makes him want to give up. The story he tells himself about the climb and his abilities to complete the task of making it to the top make it very difficult for him to accomplish and enjoy what he set out to do."

"On the other hand, the climber that has a story that serves, acknowledges the accomplishment of how far they have climbed by looking back versus looking up, and has faith that they will reach the top. Instead of getting overwhelmed at what lies ahead, he remains focused on the task, one step at a time, and enjoys the challenge. This climber most likely has a very strong desire and belief in what he's doing and what he can accomplish. I'd bet that he also understands that in order to achieve a goal, one must not get overwhelmed at the task at hand, and that the thoughts one chooses to think and believe must instill confidence, or at the very least not be negative," said Mr. Ocean.

He paused and took a drink of water.

"Do you think there's any chance the climber with the positive, optimistic outlook can help change the attitude and story of the climber with the negative, defeatist outlook?" asked Mr. Ocean.

A few hands went up.

"Yes, Justin."

"I don't think it will be easy, but I think it can be done. Just like we learned last week about being able to empower someone's thinking, like Kobe and his mom's cooking, I think the climber can also help," said Justin.

"Excellent point, Justin. Helping change someone's mindset and story they tell themselves is not always an easy task, but it can be done. People are not always receptive to change, but if you have the opportunity to change the story of someone you love into a story that serves them, I say go for it. If the story you tell yourself about your own story doesn't serve you, change it to one that does. When you do this, everything in your life will change."

What are your thoughts and most important takeaways from the chapter?

What is it about your story and the way you tell it to yourself that needs to change?

Chapter 14:

Meditation
[Auditorium]

"The benefits of meditation are numerous. To quote the 14th Dalai Lama, a very wise man and spiritual leader of Tibetan Buddhism, 'If every eight-year-old in the world is taught meditation, we will eliminate violence from the world within one generation,'" said Mick.

"Whoa, I like that. Is meditation a religious thing then?" asked Leon.

"Meditation is not associated with religion, it's something anyone can do regardless of their beliefs," said Mick.

"That would be amazing, do you think it's true? Could meditation really end all violence?" asked Viv.

"I believe so. Besides gaining more compassion and peace of mind, meditation allows you to tap into your uniqueness, which is another way of saying your own inner wisdom or superpower," said Mick.

"*Say what!* Superpower?" asked Viv.

"Yeah, you know, like Clark Kent becoming Superman, or Peter Parker becoming Spiderman," said Leon.

"Using the word superpower just sounds a little far-fetched, that's all," said Viv.

"And it sounds like someone hasn't meditated in a while and has forgotten about its many benefits," said Leon.

"Out of practice, you are," said Mick.

"Preach, Yoda," said Leon.

The audience laughed.

"When I speak of a superpower or superpowers, I'm not referring to the ability to scale tall buildings or physically fly, like some of the superheroes you know," said Mick.

"Which would be nice, though," said Leon.

"I'm referring to the ability to tap into one or more of your unique gifts that make you special. This is your inner wisdom, which is a gift you have that not only makes you come alive, but a gift you have for the world that no one else has or can do quite like you," said Mick.

"Sounds like a superhero to me," said Leon.

"Tapping into your inner wisdom or superpower requires you to listen to your inner voice, a voice that's heard by spending time by yourself in silence," said Mick.

"What? That sounds weird—spending time by yourself listening to your inner voice?" asked Viv.

"Well, you tell me, is it weird to be able to shut out the noise and distractions of this world, and tune into something that will give you more guidance, peace, confidence and self-worth?" asked Mick.

"Putting it that way, no, I guess that doesn't sound weird at all," said Viv.

And if you haven't heard, meditation is extremely good for you *and* cool to do. Celebrities, movie stars, athletes, all kinds of people do it, and it's not just a trend. It's been around for thousands of years," said Leon.

"That's correct. Meditation allows us the ability to tap into our own inner wisdom, and as we've already spoke on, what is happening on the inside will reflect what is happening on the outside. To quote the Dalai Lama again, 'We can never obtain peace in the outer world until we make peace within ourselves,'" said Mick.

"Obtaining peace and tapping into our superpower sounds pretty awesome. I think you've got our attention; you certainly have mine. So, the question is, what is meditation and how do you do it?" asked Viv.

"The definition of meditation, quite simply, is relaxed focus. It is quieting and clearing the mind, letting go of tension, and focusing on one thing, being present with what you are doing," said Mick.

"That's it? Quiet your mind, relax, and focus on one thing? That's all there is to it?" asked Viv.

"Yes. That one thing could be focusing on your breathing and shutting out everything else to the best of your ability. Or it could be bringing your awareness to your body, allowing your muscles to relax. This one thing could also be a sound you focus on, or a repeating *mantra*, or phrase you say to yourself. It could also be a thought you focus on and feel, such as love or compassion. It could even be visualizing something or gazing at an object such as a flower or a candle," said Mick.

"That doesn't sound too difficult," said Viv.

"It's like anything else. The more you do it, the easier it becomes. While there are hundreds of different types of meditations you can find in books, apps, and online, including mindfulness and visualization, this is the basic premise. Meditation is the art and science of letting go and relaxing. The letting go begins with the body and then progresses to thoughts, giving your full attention to whatever you have chosen. Meditation allows us to do that, healing ourselves, and showing ourselves the love and kindness that we truly deserve," said Mick.

"It sounds so simple, but I find it hard to focus on one thing. My mind tends to jump around all over the place, then I wonder if I'm doing it right, and then I wonder if I'm just wasting my time," said Viv.

"Those are very normal things to experience and feel, and you will find that the mind tends to wander off towards the past or the future. In meditation, it's not about controlling our thoughts and emotions; it's about not having our thoughts and emotions control us. We want to be able to be the observer of a thought when it arises, without reaction, and without judgment, and then let go of the thought and bring our focus back to our one thing," said Mick.

"That's really what it's all about. We're learning how to quiet our minds and observe our thoughts without reacting to them," said Leon.

"Yes. That, and learning how to concentrate and go deep within ourselves. Our brains are constantly stimulated with technology, and we often jump from one thing to the next, diverting our attention in many directions. Giving our focus and concentration to one thing is very powerful and something that benefits us. As a society, we're also very reactionary, meaning we often react without thinking instead of responding intelligently. And when it comes to young people, the part of the teenage brain that *feels* emotions has fully developed, yet the part that *regulates* emotions has not," said Mick.

"This must be why I've heard more than one adult say that teenagers are out of their mind," said Leon.

"*Ha!* So, it actually has some truth," said Viv.

"The fact is, self-control plays a big factor in determining the direction of our lives," said Mick.

"Really?" asked Viv.

"Yes. Self-control is more important than intelligence and social class. And in children, self-control has been known to predict physical health, personal wealth, and public safety," said Mick.

"So basically, the self-control a person displays when they're younger can predict a lot about their future," said Leon.

"Yes, it is that important, and a big reason we're here. We understand the stresses of being a young person, and we must give ourselves the tools to be able to handle stress, as well as having self-control. As you will come to find, meditation is very healing and puts us in control of how our day will unfold," said Mick.

"Makes sense. Now, as you were saying, the benefits of meditation," said Leon.

"Yes, in helping you live your best life possible, it's crucial that we discuss the power of meditation. There are mental, physical, and emotional benefits to consistent meditation. Our bodies, feelings, and thoughts are closely connected, which is why meditation affects all of these areas in a positive way," said Mick.

"Let's hear about the physical benefits first," said Leon.

"For our physical health, when we meditate, we are doing a lot of good for our bodies, and we are in tune with what our body needs. Meditation improves our energy, immune system, breathing, and heart rate. It reduces our blood pressure and stress in our bodies, and decreases inflammatory disorders," said Mick.

"Meditation does all that?" asked Leon.

"Yes, with meditation we give ourselves a chance to live longer, healthier lives," said Mick.

"I'll be looking up everything you're saying. Not that I don't believe you, but I like to fact check what I'm hearing," said Viv.

"Please do. There has been extensive research done on meditation that verifies how many benefits there are from it," said Mick.

"So basically, meditation helps our bodies be as healthy as possible. I could even become better at surfing and playing baseball just by meditating?" asked Leon.

"Yes," said Mick.

"And the problems people have as they get older that relate to the heart, stress, inflammation, blood pressure, and other areas could be reduced or eliminated just by meditating?" asked Viv.

"Yes, meditation will help your body function properly as you age. Moving on to the mental benefits of meditation, when we meditate, we also do a lot of good for our brain. Meditation increases our mental focus and strength, our memory recall, cognitive skills, creative thinking, information processing, decision making, problem-solving, and ability to be more mindful and visualize. It also helps us to ignore distractions and manage ADHD," said Mick.

"Wow. So basically, it increases our ability to focus and think, making us wiser and smarter, resulting in better grades," said Viv.

"Correct. For our emotional health, meditation does a lot, as well. It enhances our self-esteem, confidence, self-love, and acceptance. It lessens negative emotions like worry, anxiety, stress, depression, loneliness, and fear," said Mick.

"All that? Really?" asked Leon.

"Yes, really. It also increases optimism, relaxation, awareness, and it generates love and kindness towards us and others. It also improves sleep, helps fight addictions, improves resilience to pain and adversity, and improves our social lives," said Mick.

"Holy moly, that was a mouthful. So basically, meditation makes us feel better about ourselves, improves our mood and sleep, so we're happier and more content, and because of this, we're more confident, more compassionate, our communication with others improves, and our social lives get better," said Viv.

"That's right," said Mick.

"Incredible!" exclaimed Viv.

"That *is* incredible. And you mentioned that meditation helps control pain, what's that all about?" asked Leon.

"Our perception of pain is connected to our state of mind, and pain elevates in stressful situations. When we decrease stress levels in our mind and body, focus on the things that benefit us, and we're mentally, physically, and emotionally strong, we improve resilience to pain and adversity," said Mick.

"So, the slogan 'no pain, no gain' could really be know meditation, no pain, with the first know being spelled k-n-o-w. Get it? And you could reverse that as well. No meditation, spelled n-o, know pain, with the second know spelled k-n-o-w," said Leon.

"I see what you did there, clever. I like that, Leon," said Viv.

"Thanks," said Leon.

"Many problems with our health have to do with the stress that we put on ourselves, and not managing our stress levels. As mentioned, our thoughts, feelings, and physical body are closely connected. That means when we don't manage the stress that we feel, and if we continue to let it build up, this creates discomfort in our minds and bodies. This discomfort or dis-ease in the body can often lead to sickness, and even disease," said Mick.

"You're telling me that we can help prevent stress, getting sick, and in some cases, prevent diseases, just by meditating?" asked Leon.

"Yes," said Mick.

"Let me get this straight. When we consistently meditate, we become stronger and healthier in our minds, bodies, and in the way we feel, which has to do with how we manage our emotions. We tap into our own inner wisdom or superpowers. We connect with ourselves and the world around us on a deeper level, and our thoughts and feelings towards ourselves and others are, overall, much better. That's what I hear you say, right?" asked Viv.

"That's correct," said Mick.

"So basically, meditation helps heal us, and helps us become a better version of ourselves, so why isn't everyone already doing this?" asked Viv.

"Good question. Some people don't know about meditation, or they know very little about it, while others doubt its usefulness. Others have heard about it but aren't aware of how many benefits there are, while some know the benefits, but have difficulty in forming good habits," said Mick.

"Yeah, I know about the benefits of meditation and still find it difficult to meditate some mornings. There's just something about that snooze button," said Leon.

"And for me, it's not about the snooze button. It's about my phone. I love it and I can't leave it alone; it's like I'm addicted to it. Don't tell my mom, though—she might take it away from me," said Viv.

"Technology can serve you well, but make sure it's not you that's serving technology. If not done in moderation, it can take away from your relationships and self-growth. If you're like me, you charge your phone overnight, so it'll be ready for you the next day. Meditating in the morning does the same thing for your mind and body. When you take time away from your phone and distractions in order to meditate, it's like plugging yourself in to make sure you're fully charged to take on the day. That's why we meditate," said Mick.

"That's genius, Mick. And you just gave me an idea for a billboard or T-shirt. It would say, 'Devices need recharging and so do you. Meditate,'" said Leon.

"That's even better than the last phrase you just made up. Simple and easy to understand, and definitely better than most billboards or T-shirt slogans I've seen," said Viv.

"Meditation does this for you and doing it for just a few minutes in the morning instead of hitting the snooze button or immediately looking at your phone will do wonders for you. When you make meditation part of your daily routine, you are setting yourself up for greater mental, physical, and emotional health, which leads to a healthier, more fulfilled and productive you," said Mick.

"Well, I've heard enough, you can count me in!" exclaimed Viv.

What are your thoughts and most important takeaways from the chapter?

If you're not already meditating for a few minutes each day, what do you think you could cut down in your morning routine to do so?

Chapter 15:

As if It's Already Happened
[Classroom]

"What do you think happens to people that write down something they want to achieve, such as their goals?" asked Mr. Ocean.

A few hands went up and he pointed to one of the students.

"I think if they write something down and keep it somewhere they look at often, they're more likely to accomplish what they want, over someone that doesn't have anything written down. Kind of like our assignment notebook or journal," said Katie.

"Great answer Katie, and yes, that's a big part of why we use our assignment notebook, and why I have you write down our quotes in your journal. If someone has something written down they want to achieve, and they constantly look at it and work towards it, they are far more likely to succeed than someone without a written-down goal. And the more specific and clear your written-down goals are, the closer you'll come to achieving what you want."

"Class, you might have you heard me mention before, 'act as if you were already the person you most want to be' or 'live life as if everything is rigged in your favor.' Does that sound familiar?" asked Mr. Ocean.

"Yes," said the class.

"These sayings complement this week's quote about telling yourself a story that serves, as well as a trick you can do when writing something down you want to accomplish. Would you like to know what it is?" asked Mr. Ocean as he leaned in towards the class.

"Yes," said the students.

"I call this the, "as if it's already happened" trick. When you write something down you want and have a clear picture in your mind of what that is, the next part is feeling, believing, and acting as if it's already happened, combined with taking action to make it happen. Just like we learned that everything is energy, you must match the frequency and vibration of what you want, in order to make something become reality," said Mr. Ocean.

The room was silent.

"I'm going to repeat that in case you didn't quite comprehend what I just said. When you write something down you want and have a clear picture in your mind of what that is, the next part is feeling, believing, and acting as if it's already happened, combined with taking action to make it happen. If this remains your focus and desire, you will eventually match the reality you want."

Jake raised his hand.

"Yes, Jake."

"You're telling me that if I follow those steps, I can do anything I want, like make Hollywood movies?" asked Jake.

"That's exactly what I'm telling you, Jake. We have the ability to create the reality we wish to see, and a big part of that is the story we tell ourselves, along with doing the things I just mentioned, as if our goal has already happened," said Mr. Ocean.

"That's so cool, thanks, Mr. O," said Jake.

"You're very welcome. Class, in regard to changing the feelings and beliefs about the different stories you tell yourself, we have an assignment to go over."

Mr. Ocean passed the assignment out to everyone in the front row. Within a matter of seconds the papers had all been passed back and everyone had one on their desk.

"Before going over the directions for our assignment, I want to point out that this handout is on our website, "wisdombeyondtheclassroom.com." That way you can share this information with family and friends, or download and print a copy, in the event that your dog ate your homework," said Mr. Ocean.

The class laughed.

"On the assignment in front of you, titled, "A Story That Serves," you will see one side of the paper that has a circle, and inside that circle, it says, "What I Tell Myself." As you can see, this is a word web, with lines that come off the circle. Here, you will write down things you tell yourself that are positive, neutral, and negative. We have thousands of thoughts a day, so obviously what you tell yourself has a very wide range. I suggest keeping it simple, like what you tell yourself about what you do well or not so well, and how you view yourself and your relationships. Pulling from the categories of your home life, your school life, and your extracurriculars will help narrow it down. With three of these being positive, three being neutral, and three being negative, you will come up with nine of these in total. Are you with me so far? Let me get a *yep yep* if you are."

"Yep, yep," said all the students in the class, except one student that raised their hand.

"Yes, Tony."

"Mr. O, what do you mean by neutral? Is it good that something would be neutral or is it not good?" asked Tony.

"Thank you for the question, Tony, I know some of your classmates might have been wondering the same thing. When I say *neutral*, I'm referring to something that's not necessarily good or bad, it's sort of an afterthought or in the middle. You don't tell yourself something positive or negative about it and perhaps you haven't given it a lot of thought. Let me ask you, is there something you feel like you're ok at, but that you could be better at if you gave it more time and energy?" asked Mr. Ocean.

"Well, I'd say I'm pretty average at math, but I don't spend a lot of time with it. Come to think of it, I've kind of just accepted that I'm average at it," said Tony.

"Would it be fair to say that you might be selling yourself short when it comes to math? In other words, it sounds like you've accepted that you're average at math, but do you think that maybe you could be doing a lot better than you think?"

"Yeah, maybe I could. Ok, now I get what neutral means.

Thanks, Mr. O," said Tony.

"You're welcome, Tony. Class, the negative, as well as the neutral items, are the ones we want to change in your mindset, as well as reinforcing the positive beliefs you have. I will give you a positive and negative example, as well as another neutral example in just a moment. Questions so far?" asked Mr. Ocean.

A few of the students said no, and a few more shook their heads.

"Okay, after completing your word web, you will turn your paper over and notice that the title, "A Story That Serves," has three subtitles that divide the paper into three parts. On the left side, you have the subtitle, "What I've Told Myself," with the words *positive*, *neutral*, and *negative* below it. You are only writing down one for each, so choose which of the three from your word web is most important and then write that down under each category."

He waited for a few moments.

"Next, in the middle, you see the subtitle, "What I Believe and Now Tell Myself." This is where you will write your new and improved version of what you believe and now tell yourself, for your positive, neutral, and negative example. Is this making sense? Give me a thumbs up if it does, sideways thumb if it sort of does, or a thumbs down if it doesn't," said Mr. Ocean.

All the students gave a thumbs up.

"Great. Here's an example of something positive, neutral, and negative I might tell myself and write down. Of course, I'm going to put my name on my page first and then fill out my word web with nine lines, just like I *know* all of you will do," said Mr. Ocean in a dramatic tone.

The class laughed.

"My positive example of what I tell myself might be that I'm a good friend, my neutral example might be that I'm an okay sibling, and my negative example might be that I'm not popular. These, of course, are just examples. You all know that I'm most likely spectacular in all these areas."

Again, the class laughed.

"After I've written these down on the left side, with my positive example first, followed by my neutral and negative example, I will then write the new changes in the middle, as if they've already happened. As mentioned, this subtitle is appropriately named, "What I Believe and Now Tell Myself." I will reinforce my positive example and write something in the middle, like, I am a good friend because I'm caring and a good listener. You could expand this even further if you want to write something like, I am a good friend because I'm caring and a good listener, and I reach out to those that need a friend," said Mr. Ocean.

A hand went up in the class.

"Yes, Aiden."

"So, first write it on the left side, but say more about how you want it to be in the middle, so it goes from good to great?" asked Aiden.

"Exactly, Aiden. Thank you for clarifying that. Now, for the neutral example, in the middle, I can write something like, I'm putting in more time and effort, and becoming a better, more understanding sibling every day. Something I know you're all very capable of and would love to work on," said Mr. Ocean with a smile.

Laughter and the word, no, could be heard from the students.

"For the negative example, I might write something down in the middle like, I make friends easily and attract the kind of friends I want in my life. Doing so and having this kind of mentality invites more of who I want to be surrounded by, and is a lot more positive than, I'm not popular. Give me two taps on your desk if you think this can have a positive impact on what you tell yourself and what you want to attract in your life."

Everyone in the class tapped on their desk twice.

"That's music to my ears! Remember, class, *energy flows where attention goes*, especially when you write down what you want and see things in your mind as if they've already happened. When you do that and believe they will happen, and put in the work to make them happen, you create the reality you want. Now, I want you to take a few seconds, get out of your seat, stretch your body, and then sit back down. I'll give you about fifteen seconds."

The class stood up and stretched. After about 15 seconds they continued.

"Alright, on the right side of the page the subtitle is, "How Often/Action Taken." This shows each day of the week, which makes it easy for us to track whether our self-talk represents what we've written on the left side or middle of the page. When your self-talk reflects what you wrote in the middle of your page, you will put a checkmark next to the day of the week and write down the words or actions that you took. If it reflects what is on the left side of the page, you'll put an X. Your goal is to get as many check marks as you can. If you're following me, let me hear an, *all aboard*," said Mr. Ocean.

"All aboard," said the class.

"Good. Right now, I want everyone to put today's date right beside the W on the right side of the page, which stands for Wednesday. For the remaining days of the week, you don't have to put the date, just a checkmark or an X. Doing so will be an easy way for you to track your progress. Again, you want to have as many checkmarks as possible, and you want to make sure you're tracking this honestly. If you're following me, let me hear two claps."

Everyone clapped twice.

"Today is a perfect day to start changing your self-talk, the story you tell yourself, and believing in something as if it's already happened. When you do that, your state of mind and body language changes. You will have more of a belief in yourself, more courage, and more confidence. Tell me, what would someone sound like that has incredible belief, courage, and confidence? Would their growl be big or small?"

"Big," said the class.

"And what about their roar, would it be loud or soft?" asked Mr. Ocean.

"Loud!" yelled the class.

"Let's hear your best roar!"

The class let out all kinds of loud and ridiculous roars.

"That was good, now let me hear an even bigger roar!" exclaimed Mr. Ocean.

This time the class was even louder.

"*Whoa*, that was the biggest, funniest mix of roars I've ever heard!"

The students laughed.

"Some of you even got out of your chairs to roar. Justin flexed when he roared, Luke hit his chest when he let out his roar, and the look on Keisha's face made me want to run and hide!"

The class laughed even louder this time.

"What's interesting is that when your belief, courage, and confidence went up, you didn't just have a change in your mindset when you roared, most of you had a change in your body language as well. What you believed, you also felt in your body. And that's important because your body and your mind are connected. When you truly believe something, you know it to be true in your head and your heart, and you feel it in your body," said Mr. Ocean.

He paused for a moment.

"Writing something down you want, and visualizing, feeling, believing, and acting upon something as if it's already happened will benefit you for the rest of your life. The story or stories you tell yourself will change for the better. Now, you have an advantage because you're young and have been given this information at an early age. However, even if you were older, like someone your parents' or grandparents' age, a change in the story you tell yourself can still happen. Rhetorical question—what do you think would happen if you shared this information with someone? Do you think they would benefit from it?"

The students nodded their heads or said, yes.

"When you go home to work on this assignment tonight, I encourage you to share what you're doing and why you're doing it, such as with a parent, grandparent, or sibling. You very well might get them to think about their own self-talk and what changes they need to make. Why? No matter your age, you can always change the story you tell yourself to one that is serving instead of dis-serving," said Mr. Ocean.

He paused for a moment.

"This assignment will be due next week, after we've had the opportunity to track it for an entire week. Make sure you put this someplace you will see every day, so you're able to track your progress before you go to bed at night. I encourage you to be honest with what you write down, especially with your negative self-talk."

He took a deep breath and smiled.

"I appreciate the fact that you were all such excellent listeners during *Ocean's Why Wisdom Wednesday*, otherwise known as …"

"OWWW," said the class.

"Yes, OWWW. Before we move on to what we have going on next, put your pencils *down*, stand up, and shake your bodies out!" exclaimed Mr. Ocean.

If you would like a copy of the homework assignment the class is working on, it can be found online at wisdombeyondtheclassroom.com.

What are your thoughts and most important takeaways from the chapter?

What is something in your self-talk you want to change or something important for you to achieve, that you could write down, believe, take action on, and see in your mind as if it's already happened?

Chapter 16:

Mindfulness and Displaying Emotional Intelligence [Auditorium]

"We don't always have time to meditate, especially when our day has already begun, and we're around other people in social settings. In this case, we can still unplug for a few moments and hit the reset button when we need to," said Mick.

"Oh yeah, how so?" asked Viv.

"By practicing mindfulness," said Mick.

"Mindfulness?" asked Leon.

"What we refer to as mindfulness is simply being mindful or aware of something without judgment. For example, if you feel stressed about something, instead of being upset about it or continuing to feel stress, you can take a couple of deep breaths, close your eyes for a moment and tell yourself to relax and release the tension you're feeling. In this case, you're being mindful that you need a break from what you're doing," said Mick.

"Like taking a brain break instead of continuing to feel lousy," said Viv.

"Exactly. The core elements of mindfulness are the intention of why you're focusing, the attention you're giving, and the attitude you have while doing it. Mindfulness can be done throughout the day, doing practically anything. For example, you can practice mindfulness when you're eating, brushing your teeth, studying or having a conversation with someone," said Mick.

"And maybe you're mindful or aware that you're not focusing on something very well, and then it brings your attention back to what you're doing," said Leon.

"That's true as well," said Mick.

"I get it; we're really just paying attention to what we're doing, with focus and being aware of our attitude and how we feel," said Viv.

"Correct. Mindfulness is a way of being and a way of living, and mindfulness during meditation is a way to strengthen and develop mindfulness. If you are focusing on something such as your breathing and your mind drifts off during meditation, this is very normal. You simply observe when this happens without getting emotionally attached and come back to your breathing," said Mick.

"Ok, that makes sense. And what about when it comes to our emotions, like when we get upset with other people. Can mindfulness help with that?" asked Viv.

"Yes. By becoming mindful of how we are feeling, we will do a much better job of being able to respond intelligently instead of reacting without thinking. This is what emotional intelligence is," said Mick.

"So, emotional intelligence is making smart decisions when it comes to our emotions?" asked Leon.

"Correct. Emotional intelligence refers to our ability to recognize which of our thoughts to believe, the ability to choose our attitude, and have control over our actions and words. Showing emotional intelligence also has to do with recognizing the emotions of others, listening to others, and being empathetic to how others feel," said Mick.

"I've got a confession to make. Last week I got upset with my little brother and yelled at him when I shouldn't have. I was definitely not mindful and pretty much displayed no emotional intelligence. You could say I was kind of a jerk," said Viv.

"Don't be too hard on yourself, at least you recognize that you could have handled the situation better. While your brain is more developed than your brothers, your teenage brain is still developing when it comes to regulating emotion. This a good time to lay a solid foundation in strengthening your emotional intelligence, rather than waiting until you become an adult and are perhaps more set in your thoughts and beliefs," said Mick.

"I totally agree. I don't want to enter adulthood and still react based on how I feel. I want to be able to respond and have control over my thoughts, attitude and actions," said Viv.

"Yeah, I feel the same way," said Leon.

"Every time you are tempted to react in the same old way, ask if you want to be a prisoner of the past or a pioneer of the future," said Mick.

"I like that. But you gotta remember, Mick, this is still not easy to do. Most of us didn't grow up as monks, learning mindfulness and meditation at an early age like you did," said Leon.

"It's been said that life is 10% of what happens to me and 90% of how I react to it. This is true, except I like the word *respond* instead of *react*. Regardless of your circumstances or how you were brought up, you can recognize when you feel a certain way, but that doesn't mean you have to react in a way you may possibly regret later. Instead, be mindful of how your emotions make you feel. Take a deep breath, think about what you would like to say or do, and then show emotional intelligence by responding," said Mick.

"You know, that reminds me of what you said earlier about how our outer world reflects our inner world. When we react to a situation without thinking, we're usually not happy with something, and more than likely we get a reaction back we don't like. On the other hand, if we're mindful about how we feel, the thoughts we think, and can respond intelligently, we will usually get a response back that's much more pleasant than a reaction," said Leon.

"Excellent point. What we're discussing deals with emotion and self-control. We have to keep in mind that when it comes to people, we are not dealing with creatures of logic, we are dealing with creatures of emotion. Everyone on our planet has inherited an ancient and, in some ways, outdated brain. Our ancestors had immediate dangers and had to make quick decisions, usually by running or standing their ground. This is known as the fight or flight mode, and even though this model doesn't serve us like it once did, it's something our brains still have programmed," said Mick.

"Yeah, like caveman times. They were hunting for food and being hunted at the same time. All we have to think about today is take-out or delivery. Man, we got it good," said Leon.

"Meditation and mindfulness give way to emotional intelligence and the ability to be aware of our thoughts, attitude, feelings, and actions. This awareness gives us the freedom to be able to respond instead of react. We are able to feel the feeling without becoming the emotion. We can recognize that we are feeling an emotion, allow it to happen and let go of it without being attached to it. Then we can respond in a way that best serves us," said Mick.

"*Whoa*, so in a way, meditation gives our brain the upgrade that is actually needed in today's world. By using it we become more mindful and have greater emotional intelligence," said Viv.

"Yes, that's a very good way to look at it," said Mick.

What are your thoughts and most important takeaways from the chapter?

Think of a time when you reacted instead of responded. How would it have benefited you, and how might the outcome have been different if you had been mindful in displaying emotional intelligence? What part of your day could you be practicing more mindfulness?

Chapter 17:

You Are More Than Enough
[Classroom]

"Class, it's that time again. What time is it?" asked Mr. Ocean.

"OWWW time!" said the class.

"I love your energy, let's keep that good energy going. Repeat after me, I'm amazing!"

"I'm amazing!" exclaimed the class.

"Turn to the person next to you and say, you're amazing!"

"You're amazing!" shouted the class.

"Now give yourselves a round of applause."

The class clapped, a few students shouted, and one student whistled.

"Alright, that's what I'm talking about! Now, since we all have our, A Story That Serves, assignment out and completed from last week, let's go through this and give an example of one positive, neutral, and negative item. Who has an example they would like to share that's positive?" asked Mr. Ocean.

Almost everyone in the class raised their hands.

"Yes, Paulo."

"I said that I'm a good soccer player," said Paulo.

"Ahh, yes, that is certainly true. And what did you write down in the middle to reinforce this or to expand it?"

"I wrote down that I'm a good soccer player because of my passing skills, and that I'm becoming an even better player with more focused practice," said Paulo.

"That's very insightful and a good job of expanding on your positive example. And how did it go with the tracking? Did you follow through with what you wrote down in the middle of your page? Were you able to give yourself a checkmark each day?" asked Mr. Ocean.

"Yes. I looked at this every day and gave myself a checkmark for each day. I wrote down that I practiced every day, and for three of the days, I put in extra practice time," said Paulo.

"Fantastic. Keep up the good work, Paulo, and continue to keep this on your mind and in front of your eyes. What you focus on expands and will become your reality."

Paulo smiled, feeling proud of the fact that he put in extra practice and felt more confident in what he could accomplish.

"Now, who has a neutral example?" asked Mr. Ocean.

About a third of the hands went up.

"Yes, Keisha."

"I said that I'm so-so when it comes to science class," said Keisha.

"Alright, so you're *OK* in science, and what did you write down in the middle to have better self-talk?"

"I wrote down that with some extra work, and with some help from my science teacher and from my friends, I will become an A student in science."

"That's excellent, Keisha. And how did your tracking go? Did you follow through well?"

"Kind of—I gave myself five checkmarks. I forgot to look at it over the weekend and didn't ask for any help from friends, but I did look at it each weekday, and I even went in and I talked with the science teacher about what I need to work on," said Keisha.

"That's great progress, Keisha. It sounds like you're well on your way in becoming an A student. Keep up the fantastic work," said Mr. Ocean.

"Class, changing your story and self-talk, to one of belief and optimism is the progress we're looking for. What you wrote down about your negative self-talk is getting really personal and honest, and can shed light on the fact that some of your self-talk may be lousy. But guess what? That's okay. We're all human, we all make mistakes, we've all put ourselves down, and have thought things that don't serve our best interests. But how often you do this makes a big difference."

He paused for a moment.

"For your negative example, you might have put something like, 'I'm bad at this,' or 'I'm terrible at that,' 'I'm not attractive enough, not smart enough, not creative enough, not funny enough, not something enough.' Do we do that? Are we often too hard on ourselves?" asked Mr. Ocean.

"Yes," said the class.

"Pushing ourselves to do our best is different than putting ourselves down. We can be so quick to beat ourselves up mentally. If you find yourself doing this, might I suggest using a feather, not a bat."

The students smiled and Mr. Ocean pointed at the board as if he was about to reveal the next OWWW quote.

"Drumroll, please!"

The class started drumming on their desk as Mr. Ocean pulled off the orange-colored construction paper to reveal the new quote.

I am more than enough.

"I am more than enough. So true, and yet we're often so tough on ourselves and don't give ourselves the love and care we deserve. Your turn, class, repeat our new OWWW quote," Mr. Ocean directed.

"I am more than enough," said the class.

"Let me share something with you. You. Are. Enough. You are more than enough just the way you are. In fact, you're one of a kind! There may be people that look like you, act like you, or share the same ideas, but there is no one else on the planet that is just like you. Every single day you should be loving and kind towards yourself."

He continued, "It doesn't matter that you have flaws, no one is perfect! And you shouldn't feel embarrassed to let the world know who you are and what makes you unique. You may feel that by revealing your imperfections or what makes you feel vulnerable will show weakness, but it's just the opposite. Everyone is unique in their own way, and it takes courage to allow ourselves to be vulnerable and accept ourselves for who we truly are. Say it with me now. I am more than enough."

"I am more than enough," said the class.

"Okay, now say it like you mean it. Other classes should be able to hear us down the hallway. I am more than enough!" he exclaimed.

"I am more than enough!" hollered the class.

"That was better. Now this time when you say it, feel it in your bones, believe what you're saying, and say it with so much conviction that the building shakes. I am more than enough!" bellowed Mr. Ocean.

"I am more than enough!" shouted the class.

Taking a step back as if he was about to be knocked over, Mr. Ocean said, "I believe it!"

The students laughed.

"Now, take a few moments and write down the quote in your journal."

After giving the class about 20 seconds, he continued.

"Rhetorical question, class. Just like we wrote down something we want to change or work towards, don't you think it might be a good idea to write down the fact that you're more than enough and put it in a place you'll see frequently? Like your bathroom mirror, or in your notebook, or on your refrigerator," said Mr. Ocean.

There were some blank stares, and he sensed that the class had mixed feelings about this.

"Last week we talked about writing something down as if it's already happened. Whether or not you think it's a good idea to write down that you are more than enough, is entirely up to you. You can if you want, and I certainly recommend that you do, but it's not mandatory. More than anything, I want you to be able to remind yourself of how awesome you are. And to make sure you're kind and loving towards yourself every day. Keeping this in mind is important, and something too many people don't do. When you remind yourself and know that you are more than enough, it will make a difference in how you feel about yourself, your interactions with others, and your world around you. You are more than enough just the way you are."

What are your thoughts and most important takeaways from the chapter?

You are more than enough. Are you loving and kind towards yourself every day, do you tell yourself that you are enough, and are you surrounding yourself with people that believe this about you?

Chapter 18:

Visualization
[Auditorium]

As the music faded, the audience sat back down.

"Let's change subjects for a moment. By raise of hands, how many of you in here don't like public speaking?" asked Mick.

Most of the hands in the audience went up.

"And why is that? Is it because of an experience you've had? Is it because of what you tell yourself about public speaking? Is it the way it makes you feel? Or is it a combination of all three?" asked Mick.

Other than someone yelling out, all three, the audience was silent.

"When it comes to public speaking, many people fill their minds with thoughts of the speech going badly. Perhaps they think about being tongue-tied, forgetting their lines, or having a panic attack, all the while having the most unfriendly and unforgiving audience in the history of audiences," said Mick.

"That does sound terrifying," said Viv.

"However, this is just the way we perceive things, but that doesn't mean our reality can't be changed. There is power in the imagination and our ability to create what we want in our minds. What if instead, when you thought of giving a speech, you visualized or pictured yourself giving a great speech, where you completely captivated the audience, had them laughing, and on the edge of their seat. And when you finished your speech, the audience gave you a standing ovation. Imagine if you visualized that over and over, to the point where your visualization seemed and felt real. As if it had already happened. Then, do you think you'd have better thoughts and feelings towards public speaking?" asked Mick.

"I think so, but would that really work?" asked Leon.

"As powerful as the human brain is, there is a flaw, or perhaps it's just a great design that we can use to our advantage. That design is the fact that our subconscious mind cannot tell the difference between something you vividly imagine and an actual experience," said Mick.

"What are you talking about? That sounds made up," said Viv.

"Well, let's try something out to see if it's real or not. Everyone, go ahead and close your eyes for a moment. This will be a very short example," said Mick.

He paused and waited until the audience members closed their eyes.

"With your eyes closed, imagine that you are in your kitchen. You look around and notice that your kitchen looks just as it should. You turn on the kitchen light, you open and close one of the cabinets, and reach out and open the refrigerator. You see items in there, along with half of a lemon inside the refrigerator. You decide to pick it up. You can feel what a lemon feels like and see it as you hold it in your hand. You decide to give it a little squeeze, and you can smell the lemon as well. Now, without thinking about it, bite into the lemon," said Mick.

The audience reacted with a variety of noises.

"Go ahead and open your eyes. What just happened?" asked Mick.

The commotion in the audience continued, with a mixture of talking and laughing.

Leon started laughing, and Viv had a look of disgust on her face.

"OMG, my mouth is salivating, and I feel like I actually took a bite out of a lemon. Yuck," said Viv.

"You should see the look on your face—you have bitter lemon face!" exclaimed Leon as he laughed.

The audience laughed as well.

"Did it work? Did you feel like you took a bite out of a lemon?" asked Mick.

A resounding, yes, could be heard from the audience, along with a few no's.

"Sorry if that was unpleasant. It sounds like the visualization worked for most of you. If it didn't, we'll try one more example that should work, and it doesn't involve you biting into a lemon," said Mick.

He took a few steps forward.

"If you are at the end of your row, I want you to stand up. Everyone else, please continue to sit," said Mick.

He paused for a moment as audience members started to stand.

"Now, I want every other person in the row to stand so that the entire audience should have one person standing next to a person that is sitting. No two people should be standing next to each other," said Mick.

"Sit, stand, sit, stand, sit, stand, that's what your row should look like," said Viv.

Mick gave the audience a chance to comply.

If you are reading or listening to the story, and you're able to stand and try this out, go ahead and do so.

"You are all going to get the chance to do this. Leon, you do this with the first group, and Viv, you do this with the second group. Okay, for those that are standing, I want you to raise your right arm and hold it in front of you, pointing straight with your index finger," said Mick as he demonstrated this.

"Next, we're going to turn our upper body towards the right with our arm still raised in front of us. Keep your feet in place. We want to see how far we can turn clockwise, without it being uncomfortable," said Mick as he demonstrated the turn.

Half the audience turned clockwise with their arm swinging around, while half the audience sat and watched.

"Ok, for those that are standing, I want you to face forward again, drop your arm, and close your eyes," said Mick.

He paused for a moment.

"Now, without moving your body, I want you to visualize in your mind that you're picking up your right arm, with it pointed straight in front of you. Next, I want you to imagine yourself turning clockwise, but this time you can turn much further than you did the first time. You can twist all the way around as if you're an incredibly flexible cartoon character," said Mick.

Continuing, he said, "Alright, now I want you to open your eyes, raise your right arm with your index finger pointed straight, keep your feet in place, and turn your upper body clockwise."

The students that were sitting looked on as the standing students turned clockwise. As if a great magic trick had happened, every one of the students that turned clockwise went further this time. Sounds of disbelief and excitement filled the auditorium.

"Wow, that really worked!" exclaimed Leon.

"Alright, we want everyone to have a chance at this, so if you're standing, please sit, and if you're sitting, please stand," said Mick.

After the audience members got into position, Mick led this for the second group of students and got the same results. After the second group had gone, everyone took a seat.

"That was incredible. It's as if we just tricked our brain!" shouted Viv.

"Yes, but what we did was not magic; it was a straightforward exercise in visualization. Using visualization is something that top-performing athletes, actors, entertainers, and others do all the time. They are aware of how powerful the mind is and that thoughts become things, especially when you feel and believe something to be true. The more vivid you can create the image, the more often you do it, and the more you feel it, the more real it becomes," said Mick.

"So, that's it? Imagine something the way you want to see it over and over and poof, it just happens?" asked Viv.

"To some extent, yes. That also requires feeling it, believing, and taking action to make what you want a reality. The time of day makes a difference as well," said Mick.

"What do you mean?" asked Viv.

"The most effective time to influence our subconscious mind is when we're entering a much more relaxed state, such as right before we go to sleep or upon waking. Using visualization at night is a good idea because our brain waves are slowing down, and we're entering a more relaxed state," said Mick.

"Maybe so, but a lot of times, my brain's wired when I go to bed. It's like I can't shut it off," said Viv.

"What were you doing up to the point of going to bed? Did you spend some time slowing down, or were you using your brain up to the point of going to bed, like using technology?" asked Mick.

"Yeah, that's a good point. I was probably on my phone or watching TV," said Viv.

"It's been estimated that the average person has more than 50,000 thoughts a day, and of those thoughts, 90% are recycled thoughts from the previous day. So when using visualization, the belief and feelings we want to manifest before we go to sleep will carry over into the next day," said Mick.

"What?! 50,000 thoughts, *seriously*?! If that's true, how is that even possible?" asked Viv.

"The amount of thoughts someone thinks varies, but if we use that as an average, it's about 35 thoughts per minute. And if most of our thoughts are recycled, that means we're thinking the same thoughts, we're doing the same things, and we're having the same feelings," said Mick.

"Wow, like we're in a loop. Hopefully, it's a good one," said Leon.

"Like meditation and mindfulness, visualization gives us the ability to rewire our brain and how we think and feel about something, which is why repetition is key. If we can visualize or imagine something over and over, we will begin to feel it, and our subconscious mind won't be able to tell the difference between something we've visualized and a real experience. This will ultimately lead to the manifestation of what we want," said Mick.

"Wow, that's incredible. You've mentioned subconscious mind a few times—what exactly is that?" asked Viv.

"Our subconscious mind does many important things, such as keep our body functioning properly and regulate our body temperature, breathing, and heart rate. It also does what we tell it. Think of your conscious mind as a gardener, and your subconscious mind as the garden. The conscious mind or gardener is in control. The subconscious mind or garden will do as it's told. The kind of thoughts and beliefs you are planting in your mind will determine if you are producing flowers or weeds in the garden of your life," said Mick.

"Nice analogy," said Leon.

"Science suggests that our subconscious mind controls 95% of our behavior, and our behavior shapes the way we live our lives. This makes sense if you think about it, because our attitude, beliefs, and thoughts shape our lives. If you want the subconscious to work for you, give it the right requests and attain its cooperation. It is always working for you," said Mick.

"Whoa, so it really is important what we tell ourselves," said Viv.

"Yes, it is. The subconscious mind works to make our behavior fit and be consistent with how we feel about the thoughts we think and the beliefs we have. To effectively communicate ideas to our subconscious mind that will stay there, our emotions have to be genuine, meaning we have to feel and believe what we are thinking and telling ourselves. Again, the most effective times to influence our subconscious mind is either upon waking, since we've just gotten rest, or right before going to sleep, as our brain waves are slowing down and we are entering a much more relaxed state," said Mick.

"Right. And if you do this at night with self-serving thoughts, that could be good because the last thing you want to do is go to bed with negative thoughts. That would be like sabotaging yourself for hours with thoughts you don't want as you sleep," said Leon.

"Precisely. You want to go to bed with the kind of thoughts and visions that will benefit you because when you communicate your ideas and desires and feel them, they will reach your subconscious mind and shape your thoughts, beliefs, attitude, and ultimately your life," said Mick.

"And doing this will create positive momentum for the next day," said Viv.

"Yes, and this is also why starting the day off with meditation is so valuable. Along with giving you an overall sense of wellbeing and the many benefits of meditation, it helps you carry over the thoughts you have planted in your subconscious mind during visualization, which benefit you throughout the day," said Mick.

What are your thoughts and most important takeaways from the chapter?

What were the visualization examples for you like, and how can you use visualization and what you now know about your subconscious mind, to benefit you in your own life?

Chapter 19:

Comparing Doesn't Serve You
[Classroom]

"Now that we've shared a positive and neutral example, and revealed our new OWWW quote, that you are more than enough just the way you are, who is willing to be vulnerable yet courageous, and share their negative example and how well they tracked it?" asked Mr. Ocean.

No one raised their hand immediately, but after a few seconds, one hand went up.

"Yes, Leo."

"That I'm not as good as my brother," said Leo sheepishly.

"At what?"

"Like, everything. Cory's more popular. He gets good grades *and* he's a really great athlete. It's like I can't compete with him," said Leo.

"Ahhh. Yes, I know your brother Cory. In fact, I had him in my class. Maybe that's why he's so amazing," said Mr. Ocean.

The class laughed.

"Okay, Leo, what did you put in the middle of your page?"

"Well, since we're writing something as if it's already happened, and to help us change our story, I put that I'm kind to myself and don't compare myself to my brother," said Leo.

"That's really good. And how well did your self-talk go over the last week? Were you able to give yourself some checkmarks?"

"It went okay but not great. I mean, I did look at this every day, but honestly, my self-talk could have been better. I only gave myself a checkmark on three days," said Leo.

"Well, we appreciate your honesty, and that's a good start. Class, just like the three examples we've had, the harder something is to change, the more effort it will take. Our positive example got seven checkmarks, our neutral one got five, and our negative example got three checkmarks. As you can see, it's pretty important to focus and keep something in front of you that you want or need to work on," said Mr. Ocean.

He paused for a moment.

"Leo, getting back to your example with your brother, you feel like he does everything better than you, like you're living in his shadow?"

"Yeah, exactly," said Leo.

"Class, I want you to clap if you think Leo is kind to others and is a good friend."

The whole class clapped, including Mr. Ocean, and Leo smiled.

"Clap if you think Leo is smart."

The whole class, including Mr. Ocean, clapped again, and Leo smiled even bigger.

"Clap if you think Leo is funny and you're glad he's in our class."

Everyone clapped even louder, and Leo smiled ear to ear.

"Leo, you have a lot of great qualities, and so does your brother Cory. Comparing yourself to your brother or other people is ultimately a recipe for suffering, isn't it?"

"Yeah, I guess so," said Leo.

"With billions of people on the planet, there will always be someone that you could compare yourself to that you do something better than, and there will always be someone you could compare yourself to that does something better than you do. Now, I know it's hard to believe, but there are teachers in the world that are much better than I am at certain parts of our job. Can you believe it?" asked Mr. Ocean.

This got a mixed reaction of laughs, smiles, and students saying things like, yes, no way, and impossible.

"Should I focus on that and beat myself up about the fact that I'm not the best all-around teacher in the world? Apart from a little motivation to be better at my job, it won't do me any good. And if it did motivate me to be better, I would need to look at whether or not that motivation comes from a place of feeling inadequate with myself, or if it's about being better for myself and the students I'm teaching."

"A success mentality teaches not to waste energy on things that you can't change. Comparing yourself to others doesn't serve you. Go ahead and write that down in your journal, right under this week's quote, said Mr. Ocean.

After about 20 seconds, he continued.

"Let's keep in mind that comparing yourself to others, and one of our previous wisdom quotes, 'hang out with people that make you stand on your tippy toes' are two different things. Comparing means you are judging whether or not you are better or less than someone else. Hanging out with people that make you stand on your tippy toes means that you are raising your standards in whatever you're doing, without being harsh and judgmental. We've talked about this before, especially when it was our quote of the week. Who remembers an example we gave?"

A few hands went up and Mr. Ocean pointed to one of the students.

"When you hang out with people that make you stand on your tippy toes, you are hanging out with people that are good at something, and because of that, you get really good as well. Like they bring out the best in you. We mentioned that this could refer to academics, sports or a job," said Jake.

"Excellent answer, Jake. What are some other areas this could refer to?"

A few more hands went up and Mr. Ocean pointed to one of the students.

"This can also help with being creative or artistic, making money, and just being a good person," said Jocelyn.

"Exactly Jocelyn, those are also great examples. When we hang out with people that make us stand on our tippy toes, we get better and we raise our standards. That's different than comparing yourself to someone, because when that happens, you usually only feel good when you are better than someone else."

Mr. Ocean took a step forward.

"Rhetorical question, class. Do the people around you, like your family and friends, make you raise or lower your standards for yourself and what you want to accomplish?" he asked.

He let the students consider this for a moment.

"We have a tendency to be like the kind of people that we put ourselves around. The type of people that we want to be around should be those that make us raise our standards, not lower them. Who you surround yourself with is important and is certainly a reason your parents might show concern with who your friends are," said Mr. Ocean.

"Now, in getting back to our negative self-talk example, Leo, your brother is by no means perfect. No one is. For all you know, he compares himself to others and might be really hard on himself. Instead of focusing on the fact that you're not as good as your brother at something, focus on your strengths, and if there is something that your brother does better than you, think about learning from him, rather than comparing yourself to him."

He continued, "Having a good attitude in this situation and appreciating yourself will serve you best. Be grateful that you have such a cool brother, be grateful that you can learn from him, and be grateful that you are your own person, with your own strengths.

Having those kinds of thoughts will produce much better results for yourself."

"That's a good way to look at it. Now that I think about it, my brother can be tough on himself from time to time, and he really is a cool older brother. I guess it could be a lot worse," said Leo.

"Yes, much worse. Now that you know how unique and special you are, and that comparing yourself to your brother or others is generally not very healthy, what would the middle of your page say if you added to it?"

"It would say ... my brother is pretty awesome, but so am I, just in different ways," said Leo.

"Beautifully put! How about another hand for Leo, class."

The class broke out into cheers and applause.

"I'm not sure if you heard me. I said, how about another hand for Leo!" exclaimed Mr. Ocean.

As the class cheered even louder, Leo couldn't help but blush and truly felt appreciated. As the cheering and applause quieted down, Leo thanked Mr. Ocean.

"You're very welcome and thank you for the courage to share what you wrote down as your negative example, something that could make you feel vulnerable. Now, I'd like you to share what you wrote down on your worksheet, class. When I say go, if you are in row one you will turn around and take turns sharing what you wrote down on your handout with the person directly behind you in row two. Row three, you will do the same and turn around and share with the person behind you in row four. You will have three minutes. At the halfway mark, I will let you know when to switch roles between listening and talking. Ready, and *go!*"

After one and a half minutes, Mr. Ocean said, "Halfway there, switch roles."

During this time, he placed a new worksheet on the desks of every student in the front row, which would allow the students to track their self-talk over the next three weeks. After the three minutes were up, he tapped the side of his Tibetan singing bowl, which brought everyone to attention.

"Alright, rows one and three, turn back around."

He gave them a few seconds to do this.

"Thank you for sharing your self-talk examples with a classmate. If you're in row one, you'll notice that there is a new worksheet on your desk. Keep one and pass the rest behind you to row two. This worksheet has each day and date on it for the next three weeks, so that we can track our positive, neutral, and negative self-talk for one month in total. While that may seem like a long time to track something, creating lasting change takes time. We want to make sure that these changes are long-standing. Now, before you staple this to your first worksheet, I want you to find today's day and date for your positive, neutral, and negative example, and give yourself a checkmark if your story has served you and matches the middle column," said Mr. Ocean.

He gave the students time do this.

"Go ahead and staple this to the original and make sure to put it somewhere it's easy to see, like in your assignment notebook or beside your bed, and make sure you're tracking this every day. We will come back to this each week to see how well we're doing and to track the progress we've made. We'll also be writing a paper on this at the end of the month, but we'll get into the details of that later."

"OWWW time is over this morning, but we will have a new topic next Wednesday. Before moving onto Spelling and Grammar, put your pencils *down*, stand up, and shake your bodies out!"

What are your thoughts and most important takeaways from the chapter?

What's an area that you have been comparing yourself to others, and could be less judgmental of yourself or others? What's an area that you could improve upon, and hang out with people that make you stand on your tippy toes?

Chapter 20:

Combining Meditation, Mindfulness, and Visualization [Auditorium]

The music faded and the audience started to sit back down.

"Thank you. You re-confirmed that you know how to shake it!" proclaimed Viv.

"We've talked about several topics, including the benefits of meditation, mindfulness, and visualization. Are you ready to keep this adventure going and do a meditation?" asked Leon.

"Yes" could be heard throughout the audience.

"Very well then, we will move into a mindfulness meditation, which is something that many schools are using with great success. As we've mentioned, using mindfulness can be done with or without incorporating it into a meditation, and is something you can do throughout the day. However, starting the morning off with a simple mindfulness meditation is an excellent way to practice mindfulness and set the tone for how you want your day to unfold," said Mick.

"In other words, it's like activating our superpowers," said Viv.

"Precisely. In going through the meditation, if you don't feel like participating you don't have to, but please respect those in the audience, and stay quiet throughout," said Mick.

He paused for a moment, then continued.

"If you were to go into a meditation feeling tired or if you decided to lay down during it, you would likely fall asleep. You want to go into a meditation feeling strong, awake, and alert, both in your body and mind. Since your body, feelings, and thoughts are closely connected, the first thing you want to do is move your body in some way. This can be done in a variety of ways, including stretching, yoga, jumping jacks, squats, or some other form of movement or exercise. Since we just got done moving our bodies by dancing, we'll continue to the meditation," said Mick.

Mick took a deep breath as the soft, peaceful, instrumental music started to play.

"As you're sitting quietly with little movement, make sure you are sitting up tall, but relaxed and in a comfortable position ... Your feet should be flat on the ground, and your hands should be resting palms up or palms down, on your legs or in your lap, whichever you prefer ... We will start the mindfulness meditation with the intention that you're very capable of meditating, being able to focus on what will be asked of you, with an open mind and without judgment of your mind's focus, " said Mick.

As Mick looked out on the audience, he felt as if they were all connected, that they were all brothers and sisters. A sense of peace and compassion washed over him.

"As you take a deep breath in through your nose, go ahead and close your eyes ... With a long exhale, breathe out through your mouth, as if you're blowing on a hot cup of cocoa. Feel yourself relax and let go ... Take another deep breath in through your nose, and then back out through your mouth ... With the breath in, you are filling yourself up with new oxygen; with the breath out, you are releasing and letting go of any stress or tension you may be holding onto ... Take another breath in through your nose, and then back out through your mouth. Feel yourself relax and let go ... Continue breathing in through your nose, and now with the breath out, breathe out through your nose. Normal breaths now, in and out through your nose," said Mick.

He paused for ten seconds, allowing the audience to focus on their breathing.

"You should already start to feel more relaxed ... Keeping your eyes closed, bring your attention to your hands ... Notice where you have placed them ... Now, place your attention on the thumb of your left hand ... Now, place your attention on the pinkie of your right hand ... Your eyes are still closed, you are relaxed and in tune with your body ... Moving your focus down to your feet, notice that they are touching the ground ... Now place your attention on your right foot ... Now place your attention on the big toe of your right foot ... Now place your attention on your left foot ... Now on the big toe of your left foot ... Now, with your eyes still closed, go ahead and place your left hand on your tummy and your right hand on your heart," said Mick.

He paused momentarily.

"Notice the expansion of your tummy and the beat of your heart as you breathe ... Notice that your body functions just as it should, without you having to do anything."

He paused for ten seconds.

"Now, put your hands back in your lap or on your legs, and place your attention on just your breathing ... Focus your attention on your breath as it comes in and out through your nose ... Notice if you are taking in short or long breaths ... As you continue to breathe in and out through your nose, to the best of your ability, focus only on your breathing, nothing else."

He paused long enough for everyone to take three or four deep breaths.

"Notice how good it feels to breathe, and how much more relaxed you are just by being mindful of your breathing. Simple yet important. If your mind wanders, possibly thinking about something in the past or future, that's okay. It's very normal. When you notice this happening, without judgment bring your attention back to your breathing."

He paused for fifteen seconds.

"Now, with your eyes still closed, place your attention back on your hands ... Go ahead and move your fingertips ... Place your attention back on your feet ... Go ahead and wiggle your toes ... When you are ready you may slowly open your eyes," said Mick as the soft music faded.

"Wow, that was great. You guys did a fantastic job," said Leon.

"Yeah, way to go, you just learned to meditate!" exclaimed Viv.

"Not much to it, right? You start simple, meditating for a minute or so, focusing on your breathing first, and you build up from there," said Leon.

"Precisely. And how was your experience meditating? Did you find it easy? Were you able to concentrate on your hands, on your feet, and on your breathing? Take a few moments and share with the person sitting next to you what that was like," said Mick.

"We'll give you 30 seconds and let you know when you have 15 seconds left. Begin," said Leon.

The audience started talking, and after 15 seconds, Viv hollered out, switch!

After another 15 seconds, all three students clapped together five times, bringing everyone's attention back to the stage.

"That was a very short meditation and you did an excellent job. You might have noticed that when you focused on your breath, your mind may have wandered off. As I mentioned, this is very normal. Like a flowing river, we have thousands of thoughts a day. During meditation, you want to be able to observe when your thoughts occur but to do so without judgment. As if you were sitting next to a river of your thoughts, observe without getting into the river. Being mindful of that, you can then come back to whatever it is you're focusing on, such as your breathing," said Mick.

"So meditation actually helps us practice being mindful of our thoughts. And I would imagine that when we get good at it, we'll be able to recognize when thoughts come up or when something or someone causes us to feel a certain way, without actually feeling like we have to react or believe our thoughts," said Viv.

"Precisely. Meditation is not about controlling your thoughts; it's about learning how not to let your thoughts control you," said Mick.

"Beautifully put, Mick," said Viv.

"When it comes to your thoughts and emotions, by using mindfulness, you'll be able to take a deep breath, releasing any stress or tension or the need to react, instead, respond mindfully and with emotional intelligence," said Mick.

"It is incredible when you stop to think about it. We can learn to slow down and do something simple, like being aware of our breath, and by doing so, we learn about self-control. Let's do another meditation," said Leon.

"I agree, that meditation was fast, and the audience did such a great job. Whaddaya say we do one more, Mick, to give them a little more practice?" said Viv.

"And to keep everyone out of class a few more minutes. Would that be alright with you?" asked Leon.

A resounding "yes" was heard.

"I think I even heard some of the teachers say yes," said Viv.

The audience laughed.

"Alright, we'll do one more, and we'll make it a little different this time, adding in some visualization," said Mick.

He took a deep breath as he looked at the audience, and once again felt as if they were all connected, that they were all brothers and sisters. A sense of peace and compassion washed over him, and the soft, instrumental music came back on.

"As we did the first time, go ahead and fold your hands or place your hands in your lap or on your legs, palms up or palms down, whichever you prefer. Put your feet flat on the ground, sit up tall but relaxed, and with a deep breath in through your nose, close your eyes ... Take one long exhale out through your mouth, and with a nice, slow pace, begin inhaling and exhaling through your nose," said Mick.

He paused long enough for everyone to take three or four deep breaths.

"You should start to feel more relaxed and in tune with your breathing ... With the breath in, say to yourself in your mind, 're', and with the breath out, 'lax' ... Breath in, 're,' breath out, 'lax' ... With each breath in and out, you're becoming more relaxed."

He paused for ten seconds.

"Moving your attention to your hands, notice how they feel ... With your eyes still closed, go ahead and place your left hand on your tummy and your right hand on your heart."

"Notice the expansion of your tummy and the beat of your heart as you breathe ... Notice that your body functions just as it should, without you having to do anything ... Notice the strength of your heart and what a gift it is ... Feel grateful for your heart as you continue breathing."

He paused for ten seconds.

"With your hand still over your heart, think of a moment in your life you're truly grateful for ... a moment that made you feel really happy ... This might be something you accomplished that you worked hard for, being acknowledged for something you care about, or a special moment you shared with someone ... Imagine that moment and step into it, as if you're reliving it. Feel what it felt like to be back in that moment," said Mick.

He paused for fifteen seconds and the soft, peaceful music seemed to get slightly louder, as if to enhance the meditation.

"Now, think of something you're truly grateful for in your life ... It could be your home, your health, a place you've visited, or an activity you love to do ... Think of that something special and what it means to you."

He paused for ten seconds.

"Now, think of someone in your life that brings you joy, someone that loves you just the way you are ... Imagine being with that person and them telling you how special you are and how much they love you ... Imagine that you can feel and see their love pour off of them and surround you ... Notice how good that feels."

He paused for fifteen seconds.

"Now, come back to your breathing. Focus only your breath. In and out through your nose."

He paused for ten seconds.

"Take one last deep breath in and slowly release it. When you are ready, you may slowly open your eyes," said Mick.

The music faded and everyone opened their eyes.

What are your thoughts and most important takeaways from the chapter?

If you went through the meditations, what were your experiences like? If you didn't do it yet, go back and have someone read them to you, and then write about your experiences.

Chapter 21:

Your Habits Define You
[Classroom]

"Alright class, last week during OWWW time we continued discussing our self-talk, we revealed our quote that you are more than enough, and we talked about the fact that comparing yourself to others doesn't serve you. This week we have a new OWWW quote. That just feels good to say, *OWWW*. Your turn," said Mr. Ocean.

"OWWW," said the class, who instinctively laughed, smiled, or repeatedly howled the word.

"Before we reveal this week's quote, I want to thank you for being focused and staying on task this morning. Both are key in helping you achieve what you want, but you and I both know that being able to focus and stay on task is not always easy to do. In fact, it can be pretty difficult to do consistently."

He paused for a moment.

"Which leads us to our new quote. Drumroll, please!"

Anticipating this, the students eagerly tapped on their desks. Mr. Ocean pulled off the orange-colored construction paper and revealed the new quote.

Your habits define you.

"Your habits define you. Very true, and very important. As a class, let's say it together."

"Your habits define you," said the class.

"Go ahead and write that down in your journal," Mr. Ocean directed.

He gave the students enough time to write and then continued.

"So, what does that mean to you, and why is it important?"

A few hands went up and Mr. Ocean pointed to one of the students.

"This is important because depending on whether you have good habits or not will make a difference in how much you get done," said Luke.

"How so?" asked Mr. Ocean.

"Well, if you are in the habit of getting the things done that you need to get done, like your homework or chores, then you have time to do other things you like doing. But if you're in the habit of playing first, then you will most likely not be giving enough time to do the things you have to do, and then you might not do these things as well as you should," said Luke.

"That's a really good point, Luke. Who wants to add to that? Yes, Laura.

"I've gotten in the habit of doing my homework right after I get home, and it's made a big difference. Actually, my mom got me in the habit of doing this, and I'm glad she did," said Laura.

"Excellent, tell us more about that."

"I used to come home and watch TV and talk on the phone, and then I didn't have a lot of time to do my homework before going to bed. I'd end up going to bed kind of late because I waited too long to start my homework, and then I wouldn't get as much sleep as I needed, and then I'd wake up tired and grouchy."

"So, you were in the habit of waiting to do your homework and that was hurting you the next day?"

"Yeah, and because it wasn't working very well, my mom made me start doing my homework right after school and it's been really good. My work gets done a lot better and I actually feel more rested in the morning," said Laura.

"Great example, Laura. So, class, habits can be good and bad, or somewhere in the middle. Here's a great quote that goes along with habits that I'd like you to write down in your journal," said Mr. Ocean.

He turned off the lights, turned on his computer, and his screen was projected on the whiteboard, showing this:

Watch your thoughts, they become your words,

Watch your words, they become your actions,

Watch your actions, they become your habits,

Watch your habits, they become your character,

Watch your character, it becomes your destiny!

After Mr. Ocean read this aloud, the students wrote it down in their journals.

"Your habits come from your actions. Your actions come from your words, and your words come from your thoughts. These then form your character and your destiny. This is another way of saying that all of these important parts define the kind of person you are, the way you live your life, and where it's headed. We'll spend more time on this later in the year, but I wanted to introduce it to you now because it points out the importance of your habits. Regarding organization or productivity, who has another example for us when it comes to habits?"

A few hands went up.

"Yes, Niyah."

"Well, being organized isn't my best quality, as everyone knows," said Niyah.

She glances around the room and gets smiles, nods, and a few laughs from her classmates.

"I guess you could say I'm not in the habit of being organized, and I think that probably messes with how productive I am," said Niyah.

"Ok, so what do you think you could do to change that? Do you think that if you make some changes, you will gain something from it, like in Laura's example of getting more sleep?"

"I think that if I want to be more organized, it's something I need to think more about and what I will gain from it. Then, I need to take the time to make sure my desk, my papers, my notebooks, and my room is cleaned more often. Maybe do it every day, like at a certain time, and then it won't pile up and I won't lose things so often. And then if I do it regularly enough, it might turn into a good habit," said Niyah.

"So, you think if you just spend a couple extra minutes on this each day, this will make a difference?" asked Mr. Ocean.

"For sure. And it would probably make me feel more organized in my head, so I could think about other things and be more productive," said Niyah.

"Absolutely. And do you think it would make a difference if you tell yourself how well you can or can't stay organized?"

"Yes. I think it would help if I tell myself I'm good at being organized," said Niyah.

"As we've talked about before, what you tell yourself *does* make a difference, especially when you feel it, and you believe it," said Mr. Ocean.

"Yes," said Niyah.

"So, how do you make sure that you stay consistent and do a few minutes of organizing each day? That this habit is something you not only start, but continue to do each day, so that in a month, six months, or a year or more from now, you're still doing this?"

"Ummm, well, that's a good question ... I could probably write it down in my assignment notebook to remind myself to do it at a certain time of day so that it's a planned event. Just like it is a planned event when I have to be somewhere at a certain time, like my volleyball practice," said Niyah.

"Excellent answer. Your notebook or daily planner works well. You could also use your phone's calendar or alarm as a daily reminder for the things you need to do. Anything else?"

"Well, I like to use sticky notes. I could also put a couple of sticky notes up in places to remind myself. Just in case I don't look at my notebook," said Niyah.

"Yes! Using a prop such as a sticky note and placing it somewhere you will see it is a great way to remind yourself. To start out with, using a daily planner and props will help a lot, especially in the beginning when forming good habits is most difficult. Another example of a prop is using an object that reminds you of something you need or want to do and putting it in a good spot. For example, if you have a hard time waking up and getting to school on time, do you want to place your alarm next to your bed or away from your bed, class?"

"Away," said the class.

"Exactly. Don't place your alarm next to your bed where it's easy to hit the snooze button. Place it across the room where you have to get up to turn it off. Here's a few more examples. If you have a hard time remembering to floss, place the floss next to your toothbrush. If you have a hard time remembering to eat breakfast or get all your books in your backpack before school, place your books in your backpack the night before, and put your bag in the kitchen. If you want to read at night but have a hard time doing so, place a book on your bed in the morning after you've hopefully made your bed. I'm sure all of you are making your bed every morning, aren't you?"

This got a mixture of laughs, groans, "no's", and a few "yes's" from the class.

"I know making your bed in the morning is probably something a lot of you don't do or don't like to do, but when you make your bed, it starts you off with a good habit, and gives you a sense of having already accomplished something in the morning. It also allows you to start building upon your accomplishments right away, something known as *habit stacking*," said Mr. Ocean.

He paused for a moment.

"Habit stacking could look something like this. In the morning, you wake up right away without hitting the snooze button because you have to get out of bed to turn your alarm off. You make your bed, then place a book on it, which prompts you to read before you go to bed. Next, you brush your teeth, floss, and get ready, which is quick and easy because these items have already been set out from the night before. You spend a few minutes stretching and meditating or thinking about how you want the day to unfold, followed by breakfast. Finally, on your way out the door, you grab your backpack, which already has all your books placed in it from the night before."

He continued, "That is a successful and productive, boss-like morning filled with good habits, where you're already feeling very good, very confident about yourself and what you've accomplished, and what else you're going to accomplish throughout the day. And that looks and feels a lot better than going through the motions of just barely getting to school on time, looking like you just rolled out of bed with your hair sticking up and sleep still in your eyes."

The students looked around the room and some started to laugh. There were a few students that did in fact look like they had just gotten out of bed.

"Getting back to what Niyah has been saying, if she has mornings like these, it will help her become more organized and productive because she's formed better habits. We've talked a little about this before with one of our previous OWWW quotes, 'Self-discipline equals self-love.' When you do the things you need to do every day, you are taking care of yourself the way you should. Creating good habits and stacking good habits together will make you more productive and successful in all areas of your life."

Niyah raised her hand.

"Yes, Niyah," said Mr. Ocean.

"I want to add one thing to that, if you don't mind," said Niyah.

"Sure, be my guest."

"With everything we learn in here, it made me realize that sometimes I have a lousy attitude. I figured I could do something about that, so recently I've been wearing a bracelet I love with little bears on it that says, 'grateful.' It helps remind me that, whether I'm doing something I like or don't like, I have a lot to be grateful for and I get to choose my attitude. So, it has kind of become a habit of mine. You know, to be grateful," Niyah explained.

"That is a very good point and your bracelet is a great prop—thanks for sharing that, Niyah. And thank you for your fantastic examples," said Mr. Ocean.

"You're welcome," said Niyah with a big smile on her face.

"Class, along with the habit stacking that you start to form with your actions when you get out of bed, you should also start to form good habits in your mind, just as Niyah has done with her bracelet. Here's a rhetorical question for you. What would happen, if instead of dreading the morning when your alarm went off, you woke up and put your feet on the ground, smiled, and said to yourself, 'I'm amazing and more than enough, I have so much to offer, and so much to be grateful for today.' Do you think that would make a difference?"

The students stared back at Mr. Ocean, and some nodded yes.

"If you did that every morning, even before you turned off your alarm, it would become part of your habit stacking, and would make a big difference with how you start the day."

Andre raised his hand.

"Yes, Andre?"

"Telling myself I'm amazing and more than enough in the morning sounds nice and all, but Mr. O, I'm half asleep and grouchy. As the very first thing that goes through my head, that's a little too positive for me. Something like, I hope to survive the day, not argue with anyone, and find something to wear that's clean is probably more realistic," said Andre.

The class laughed.

Smiling, Mr. Ocean said, "Andre, I completely understand, and I think we've all felt that way before. I know I have. Just getting up and starting the day can be a task in itself. We all have mornings where we feel the way you just described, but make sure you're not selling yourself short."

He paused long enough for Andre to ask him what he meant by this.

"Remember, we become our habits. We want to be doing things that help us be productive, things that help us activate our body and our brain. This is the same reason we work on our self-talk and the same reason we meditate, as well as get our bodies moving before we meditate."

He slowly paced in front of the classroom.

"If you consistently have good habits in the morning and change your mindset, eventually your mindset of just surviving the day and finding something to wear will go away and be replaced with thoughts, words, and actions that serve you much better. And why is that, Andre?" asked Mr. Ocean.

"I don't know, I guess my attitude would change," said Andre.

"Yes, exactly. Your habits aren't just in the actions you take. They are in the thoughts you think and the words you speak. Keep this in mind, class. You. Become. Your. Habits."

After a moment, he continued, "I thank all of you for being good listeners, and thank you, Luke, Laura, Niyah, and Andre, for speaking up. How about a round of applause for their participation."

The class gave a round of applause and all four students smiled. While the students were clapping, Mr. Ocean started to pass out papers to each student in the front row, who then took one and passed the rest to the second row.

"Just like we wrote down and tracked our self-talk using a word web, we're also going to do that with our habits for the next week. As you can see, this paper has the same format you used for your assignment, A Story That Serves. Using the word web, you will come up with three positive habits, three neutral habits, and three negative habits you have. Out of those three for each, you will choose only one positive, one neutral, and one negative habit to work on. You will then write those down on the other side of the page, on the left side. In the middle, you will write down what you will do to improve it, which we've labeled, 'My Super-Charged Habits'. On the right side, we'll track it with a checkmark, just as we did before. Any questions on that?" asked Mr. Ocean.

The class was silent.

"We've had a few examples of how to form better habits, and about stacking good habits, but let me give you an example of one positive, neutral, and negative habit for the sake of our assignment. If you were in the habit of getting your schoolwork done when you get home, this would be a positive habit. To reinforce it, in the middle of your page you could write something like, I get all my schoolwork done immediately after school and I double check my work to make sure it's completed and satisfactory. If when your mom or dad asks for help around the house and you sometimes complain, you could put this down as a neutral habit. In the middle of the page you could write something like, I don't complain if I'm asked to help around the house. If you have trouble getting up on time, and tend to hit the snooze button every day, you could put this down as your negative habit. In the middle of the page, you could put something like, I have moved my alarm away from my bed and get up immediately without hitting the snooze button. Got it? If you're with me on this and understand, clap twice."

The students all clapped twice.

"I know you might want to use these examples on your worksheet, and I'm not saying you can't, but I want you to put some thought into these habits. You want to continue with good habits and be able to recognize an okay and bad habit that you need to work on. Do you know why that is?"

"Why?" said the students.

"Because you become your habits and being an adult that picks their nose is not cool," said Mr. Ocean as he pretended to put his finger up his nose.

The class burst out laughing.

"And neither is being someone with very little self-control, or someone that is constantly late, forgetful, or rude to others. Make sure your habits are taking you where you want to go. If you don't, rest assured they will follow you into adulthood. Now, put your pencils *down*, stand up, and shake your bodies out!"

If you would like a copy of the homework assignment the class is working on, it can be found online at wisdombeyondtheclassroom.com.

What are your thoughts and most important takeaways from the chapter?

What kind of habits have you formed in your thoughts, words, and actions that need to change?

Chapter 22:

Take "Try" Out of Your Vocabulary
[Auditorium]

Along with everyone else in the auditorium, Viv and Leon had also been participating in the meditation with their eyes closed. When they opened their eyes, they both turned to Mick and smiled.

"Mick, that was awesome, thanks," said Leon.

"Yeah, thank you. I feel so relaxed and clear-headed, like I'm the one that's in control of my thoughts and feelings," said Viv.

"And the part about the gratitude was really cool," said Leon.

"You're welcome. I'm glad you both enjoyed it," said Mick with a smile.

Mick turned his attention back to the audience.

"I want to thank you for doing such an excellent job listening and focusing during the meditation. By doing so, you gave yourself the great gifts of practicing mindfulness, gratitude, self-healing and self-love, something we should do for ourselves every day. You also allowed your classmates to experience these gifts by being respectful and quiet throughout the meditation, so thank you," said Mick.

"You have been a fantastic audience, and since our time is almost up, we want to give you the stage. What questions or comments do you have for us that we haven't answered?" asked Viv.

The audience was silent, and no one raised their hand immediately. Finally, one of the teachers in the front raised her hand, and Mick pointed to her and nodded.

"It takes guts to speak in front of a lot of people, especially when those people are at one of your rival schools. You three did an excellent job," said the teacher.

"Thank you," said Viv, Leon, and Mick together.

"I have two questions for you. My first question is how long have the three of you been speaking to students, and the second question is whether or not you always use the instrumental music during meditation," said the teacher.

"Thank you for the questions. The three of us had the idea of teaching other students ever since we were in 8th-grade homeroom together. That was three years ago. Our homeroom teacher then, Mr. Ocean, taught us most of what we've shared with you today," said Viv.

"Yeah, we knew that it was valuable information, and we also knew that the wisdom he was sharing was not something most students get the opportunity to learn. With his help, we came up with some good ideas to share, and we started rehearsing together," said Leon.

"To answer your second question, we usually use music when leading a meditation, but music is not needed when meditating. I prefer silence when meditating on my own but either one is fine," said Mick.

"Wonderful, please continue to do what you're doing. Alright, Lincoln High, I know you're not shy and that some of you have questions for our three new friends here, so ask away," said the teacher.

A few hands started to go up in the audience.

Pointing towards the middle of the audience, Viv said, "Yes, you, with the glasses and green shirt on."

"First off, I have a new appreciation for Central High students," said the girl.

This got a reaction and some laughs from the audience.

"I also want to thank you. I've never meditated before and that was powerful. I wasn't sure if I'd be able to, but you made that easy. My question is for you, Mick. If I'm a visitor, and you're a visitor, and we're all visitors, why are we here? I mean, like, what's the point of all of this?" asked the girl.

"Excellent question. And I'm pleased to hear that you have a new appreciation for Central High students, and that you had a powerful experience for your first meditation. To answer your question, why are we here, this is a question that people have been asking throughout history. There may be reasons we are here that are beyond our understanding. We don't know everything there is to know. People have determined that we are here for many reasons, while some believe that there is no point at all. The way you answer this question for yourself, though, through the way you live and view life, will determine what kind of life you will live and how fulfilling it will be. Shall I continue?" asked Mick.

"Please," said the girl.

"Since you're asking for my opinion, I believe that we are here for a few reasons. I believe that we are here to follow our own path. To connect to our inner wisdom that's unique to each of us and share that gift with the world. That we are here to evolve, learn, heal, and grow to the best of our abilities. That we are here to celebrate, appreciate, and enjoy our lives, take care of our planet, and look after all living beings. I believe we are also here to love ourselves and one another and bring joy to others. We are also here to give, supporting and serving others on their path, to recognize that we are each a miracle, and that life is a gift. And to live our lives that way every single day. Does that answer your question?" Asked Mick.

"Yes, yes it does, thank you."

"You're welcome."

"Alright, someone else. Yes, you in the grey sweatshirt," said Leon, pointing towards the back of the audience.

A boy at the back of the audience stood.

"Mick, do you really have six toes?" asked the boy.

Half the audience erupted in laughter, while the other half was shocked at the question.

"I do. Six toes on each foot," said Mick smiling.

"Can I see them?"

More laughter.

"We don't have time for that right now, but if we ever run into each other outside of school, I'll show them to you if you want."

"Deal!" said the boy, sitting down and looking pleased with himself.

The audience laughed again.

"Any other questions? Yes, you," said Viv, pointing to a boy already standing.

"Hey, thanks a lot, I enjoyed what you all had to say, and I liked the meditation. My question is also for Mick, and it's about the visualization. That was cool what you had us do with the lemon and then when we turned around. I want to start using visualization, but how much do I have to do? Like, how long is it going to take until I see results?" asked the boy.

"That's a great question, and I'm glad you asked about that. It's common knowledge that the more you do or practice something, the better you become at it. Visualization is no different, and what's important to keep in mind is feeling what you visualize. The more you feel it, the more faith you develop in what you are visualizing, and the more you do this, the more your head and your heart become aligned to know this as truth, as if it's already happened. As mentioned, when you visualize with feeling, you're sending thoughts to your subconscious mind. When you do this often enough, your subconscious can't tell the difference between these visualizations and something that has already happened. The more you do this, the more likely it is to reach and stay in your subconscious, turning your thoughts and visualizations into physical action, and eventually into your physical reality," said Mick.

"Okay, so if I want something, I need to make this a priority and use visualization often," said the boy.

"Yes. And I would recommend writing down what you want. You can get clearer on what you want if you add specific details and have it in writing," said Mick.

"Alright, thanks a lot."

"You're welcome."

"Okay, someone else. Yes, you, the girl there in the striped shirt," said Leon.

"I just want to thank you three for getting us out of class!" said the girl.

The audience agreed as many started to cheer.

She continued, "I liked the meditation and what you had to say. My question is, knowing myself, I'll try and do the meditation on my own and probably forget a lot of it. Do you guys have some information or a website that I can go to, so I remember how it goes?"

"I'm glad you liked the meditation, and as far as getting you and everyone here out of class, you're welcome. To answer your question, the answer is yes, we do have a website. If you go to wisdombeyondtheclassroom.com, you will find information, including the meditation we did today, along with a few other items."

"Thanks, I'll check it out," said the girl.

"If you don't mind, I also want to address the fact that you said the word, "try." Could I talk to you and everyone here about that for a moment?" asked Mick.

"Um, sure," said the girl.

"Thank you. If you want to try out the meditation on your own, that's fine, but the word "try" indicates that you may or may not make a great effort and that you are giving yourself a way out. If I said that I would "try" to do something rather than "I will" do something, that's a big difference," Mick explained.

"Oh yeah, anytime I say I will try to do something, there's a pretty good chance it might not happen," said Leon.

"Precisely. Let's use an example. If you're a basketball player and want to become a better free throw shooter, telling yourself that you will 'try' to shoot 100 free throws a day is much different than saying you 'will' shoot 100 free throws a day," said Mick.

"That's true," said Viv.

"It would be wise to take the word "try" out of your vocabulary. If you want to incorporate something into your life that's important to you, then you have to make it a habit and a priority. It has to become something that is part of your routine, just like I hope brushing your teeth and taking a shower is part of everyone's daily routine and not just something we try to do," said Mick.

A few laughs were heard from the audience.

"Thank you for being a good sport about using the word try," said Mick.

"Sure. And thanks for the information about the website; I'll do more than just try, I will take a look at it," said the girl in the striped shirt.

"Another question or comment. Yes, you," said Viv, pointing to the right side of the audience.

A boy stood up with a cast on his arm.

"I would love for you three to sign my cast. Can you do that?" asked the boy.

Leon and Viv turned towards Mick.

"Sure. When we're done, come on up and we'll sign it," said Mick.

"Awesome, thanks!"

"Alright, we've got time for one more question or comment. Yes, you," said Leon, pointing to a girl in the second row.

"I want to thank you three for being here today. My parents work all the time and are stressed out a lot. I think they could use some of what you taught here today, especially the meditation. Thank you," said the girl.

"You're welcome. I hope your parents benefit from what you've learned. I know they will if they listen to what you have to say. You can also refer them to our website. The information that was shared with you today, this wisdom beyond the classroom, is meant for students as well as adults. Whether you're an adult or a kid, we all make mistakes and there's always something to learn, so to some degree we are all students, regardless of one's age," said Mick.

What are your thoughts and most important takeaways from the chapter?

What 'try' do you need to take out of your vocabulary, and what questions do you still have when it comes to meditation, visualization, and mindfulness, or anything else you've learned? Write down what you will stop saying 'try' to, as well as any questions you still have, and then share these with a family member or friend.

Chapter 23:

Failure Is Part of Success
[Classroom]

The following Wednesday in Mr. Ocean's class, after students paired up and shared their, A Story That Serves and Habits worksheets, Mr. Ocean addressed the students.

"As we continue to work on our self-talk and habits, we are nurturing the seeds that we have planted in our minds. The more we nurture, the more successful we become at controlling and mastering our thoughts, beliefs, feelings, words, and actions. You are learning what works for you and what doesn't work for you, and you are learning how to make your mind your greatest asset."

He paused for a moment.

"Believe it or not, you are lifelong learners. Your learning will not stop after school, and in fact, your learning and growth will be an important part of giving you fulfillment and happiness throughout your life. So, my question to you is, what's the best way to learn something?" asked Mr. Ocean.

A few of the students raised their hands.

"Yes, Jamar."

"I think the best way to learn something is to learn from other people who have already done something you want to do," said Jamar.

"Yes, that's very true. And not just from anyone, but someone that has had success in what you want to accomplish. That's why we have coaches, teachers, and mentors, and why we read books, listen to audios, and watch informative videos," said Mr. Ocean.

"We also learn how not to do things from others that have failed," said Jamar.

"That's correct, and an excellent point. Thank you, Jamar. Someone else? What's another way to learn?"

Even more students raised their hands this time.

"Yes, Jie."

"We learn by trying something new," said Jie.

"Yes. We most certainly do. We seem to learn the most when we get out of our comfort zone, don't we?"

Some of the students nodded their heads.

That's a good intro into this week's OWWW quote. Without further ado, drumroll, please," said Mr. Ocean.

The students immediately started drumming on their desks as Mr. Ocean pulled apart the Velcro on the orange construction paper, revealing the new quote.

Failure is part of success.

"Failure is part of success. All together now," said Mr. Ocean.

"Failure is part of success," said the class.

"As you write that down in your journals, think about why this is worthy of being one of our quotes."

He paused long enough for the students to write, then continued.

"What are your thoughts on this?"

After a couple of moments, a few of the students raised their hands.

"Yes, Corinna," said Mr. Ocean.

"I think it's one of our quotes because we actually learn when we don't get something right. Like, when we mess something up, we learn the right way and the wrong way to do something," said Corinna.

"What I hear you say is that we learn from our failures. Is that correct, Corrina?"

"Yes, Mr. O.," said Corinna.

"Very good. I see that you had your hand up. Go ahead, Alyona."

"We talk about our attitude a lot. I think it's important that when we fail at something, we have a good attitude about it. We shouldn't think of failing as a bad thing, but as a good thing," said Alyona.

"Okay, and why is that?"

"Because we're one step closer to learning how to do something a better way and get it right," said Alyona.

"That's an outstanding perspective, Alyona, and I completely agree. We must develop a healthy relationship with our failures. Our failures provide an opportunity to learn. When we fail at something, we should take it in stride and with a good attitude. To reflect and perhaps even write down what we learned from a failure is a good idea. Someone else?"

A few hands went up.

"Yes, Kristy," said Mr. Ocean.

"I think failure is part of success because as long as you keep going, you're going in the right direction. If the quote said that giving up was part of success, that wouldn't make any sense. Failure just means you're learning along the way to becoming successful," said Kristy.

"Excellent answer. Did you hear what Kristy said, class? Failure and giving up are two entirely different things. Failure is part of you going down the road to success and giving up means you completely stop going down the road. And what happens then? What happens if you've gone down the road, but don't reach your destination?"

A few of the students raised their hands.

"Yes, Colleen," said Mr. Ocean.

"Well, if that happens, you've probably settled for something less than you're capable of. Which could be like saying you've given up on yourself or on your dreams," said Colleen.

"That's a very good point. The difference between someone accomplishing their dreams or not could simply be giving up after failure, instead of learning from one's mistakes." We have time to hear from one more student."

A few hands went up.

"Yes, Reed," said Mr. Ocean.

"My mom has a good saying about failure. She says that failure just means you get the opportunity to do something again with more knowledge," said Reed.

"What a great saying, and so true. Did you hear that, class? Failure means you get the opportunity to do something again with more knowledge. And when you do this, what happens? You learn, you get better at something, and you expand your comfort zone of what you're capable of. Thank you, Reed, and thank you, Reed's mom."

The class laughed.

"No matter where someone comes from, what they look like, what their ethnicity is, or how much money they have, I would be willing to bet that the most successful people alive today, and those we've learned about throughout history, all had many failures that they had to endure and learn from. The first thing successful people do is view failure as a positive signal to success. One of my favorite stories of someone doing this that still affects us today comes from the great American inventor, Thomas Edison. Edison is known for creating the first commercially practical, incandescent electric light bulb. You might have known that, but did you know that he failed thousands of times before getting it to work?" asked Mr. Ocean.

The look on the students faces was that of surprise and shock.

"How many of us today would keep going, after failing thousands of times? How many of us would learn from our mistakes, keep a positive attitude, continue taking action, and remain focused after that many failed attempts?"

The class remained silent.

"Thomas Edison was quoted saying, 'I have not failed. I've just found 10,000 ways that won't work.' Talk about desire, belief, and a great attitude! He also said that, 'Genius is 1% inspiration and 99% perspiration.'"

"How many of you, when you get home, have Mom or Dad ask you what you learned at school?"

More than half of the students raised their hands.

"Do you want to confuse your parents the next time they ask this question?" asked Mr. Ocean.

"Yes," said the class with enthusiasm and a bit of laughter.

"The next time they ask this question, start off by telling them about something you failed at in school. For example, the dialogue could go something like this. *Mom*: 'Hey honey, what did you learn in school today?'" said Mr. Ocean in a higher tone.

Laughter rippled through the classroom.

"*You*: 'So much, I learned how to fail. I really struggled with a math problem and even failed at it six times in a row,'" said Mr. Ocean.

This brought more laughter.

"Your mom might be perplexed by this, but we won't keep her in the dark too long. If the dialogue continued, it might go something like this. *Mom:* 'You failed at a math problem six times in a row?'" *You:* 'Yes, I did, but what I learned from it was how to do the problem correctly, and I kept a great attitude the whole time. I also learned that I need to check my work and not rush through it,'" said Mr. Ocean.

He paused for a moment and a few students laughed, while many of the students were smiling.

"So, if you start telling Mom or Dad something you failed at every time they ask what you learned at school, they'll eventually catch on and ask what you failed at, instead of what you learned. Does that sound fun and something you'd be willing to do?"

A resounding "yes" could be heard from the class.

"Excellent. Do this over the next few weeks, and we'll circle back to see how it's gone for you. My guess is that it will create a change in thoughts about failure for both you and your parents, which is part of having a growth mindset. In a growth mindset, challenges are exciting rather than threatening. So rather than thinking, oh, I'm going to reveal my weaknesses, you say, wow, here's a chance to grow.

When you fail at something, I want you to start thinking of it as an opportunity to learn, get better, and expand your limits and comfort zone, because failure is part of success."

"Now, put your pencils down, stand up, and shake your bodies out!" exclaimed Mr. Ocean.

What are your thoughts and most important takeaways from the chapter?

Since failure is part of success, could you have a different, more healthy perspective on your relationship with failing? What sticks out in your mind about lessons you've learned from some of your failures?

Chapter 24:

Follow Your Own Path
[Auditorium]

"Today, we covered a lot of topics that will benefit you greatly, now and in the future," said Leon.

"And most of these topics are probably not talked about and shared at home or school, but you can help to change that. It's important that you have this information and use it," said Viv.

"Yes, that is true. This information to guide you along your path is not often shared at home or school. This is not to take anything away from our home life or our education system—to guide and educate young people is a tremendous responsibility that parents and schools take on and they do the best they know how to do," said Mick.

"Yeah, following your path is really what it's all about, but doing so in an intelligent way, like using the wisdom we've shared," said Viv.

"Very true. To assist you on your path, the information we've discussed will certainly help guide you, and connecting to your inner wisdom will be important for many reasons, especially when it comes to knowing where your path should lead," said Mick.

"Yeah and that's important because there are a lot of paths to take. You might be graduating this year and will be faced with a lot of decisions that will shape the direction your life takes. And if you're not graduating, you still have choices about how you spend your time, who you spend your time with, and what to focus on. We've provided plenty of information to help everyone here along their path, but is there anything else you want to add about this, Mick?" asked Leon.

"Yes. Throughout the different chapters of our lives, there will be decisions to make, and challenges and obstacles to overcome. It will be up to us to decide how we face these. Having many choices about what to do and where to go is exciting, yet it can also be overwhelming if you don't have some direction and a goal in mind. Rather than choosing to feel overwhelmed, decide to have an attitude that will serve you best, and the point of view that you have the opportunity to choose your own adventure. In choosing this adventure, if you are faced with multiple options and are deciding which path to take, might I suggest writing down the pros and cons of each. If you have an outcome or goal in mind, writing down what you want, and having a plan of how to get there will also serve you well," said Mick.

"That's definitely great advice. Keep going, Mick," said Viv.

"To follow what seems best for you will most likely require help and guidance, which you'll get along the way. This advice may come from an unexpected source when you least expect it, but more often than not it will come in the form of one or both parents, a teacher, a mentor, a coach, a neighbor, friends or family members. It would be wise to listen to those that care and love you, as well as those that have experience in what you want to achieve," said Mick.

"Also great advice, anything else?" asked Viv.

"While you want to listen to those that care about you, that are wise and give sound advice, you also want to follow what you know is right for you. There will be times when what you feel is the right thing to do isn't the most popular decision, and it may go against what others want. That's quite alright, that is going to happen. Often times we place too much value on what others think of us, and do what others think we should do, even when it doesn't feel right or align with who we are. This is especially true when advice, opinions, or judgments come from those that don't have our best interests in mind. If you find this happening, here's a suggestion. Stop letting people who do so little for you control so much of your mind, feelings, and emotions," said Mick.

"Wow, spoken like a true "Jedi Master." Thank you wise friend, that's some good stuff you just laid down. And I guess the same could be said about the decisions another person makes and how we feel about those decisions. What is best for someone else and the decisions they make is not something we always have to agree with either," said Leon.

"True. You will not please everyone all the time and you shouldn't look to do so. The same is true for the actions and decisions of others. You have your own path to journey down, and so does everyone else. The way you decide to live your life every day is ultimately up to you, not anyone else. Whether you choose to listen to the advice of others or not, you are responsible for the actions you take and the decisions you make," said Mick.

"That's for sure. And remember, you were no accident—you are 1 in 400 trillion. You are a miracle, and there is nothing you can't accomplish. Your journey and the way you live your life should be a great expression of who you are. You can make your life a masterpiece," said Viv.

"That's right, Viv. Life is either a daring adventure or nothing at all," said Leon.

What are your thoughts and most important takeaways from the chapter?

What changes, big or small, could you make if the path you are on doesn't align with how you feel or where you want to go?

Chapter 25:

Attitude of Gratitude
[Classroom]

"Alright class, we had another week to track our self-talk and habits, and last week we talked about the fact that failure is part of success. I know you've most likely given this some thought over the last week, so let me ask you, what are you going to be successful at because you've failed along the way? If you'd like to share, please raise your hand and we'll go around the room," said Mr. Ocean.

Everyone in the class raised their hands.

"Okay, since everyone raised their hand, we'll go around the room and you can share in a *word or two*. That way we'll hear from all of you and move quickly. Ready? Alright, here we go."

He pointed to the first student.

"World-class photography," said Regina.

"Or three words," said Mr. Ocean.

The class laughed and they continued on.

"Surfing," said Niyah.

"Guitar," said Leo.

The responses varied greatly and included sports, martial arts, musical instruments, art, business owner, gardening, writer, doctor, internet guru, architect, acting, yoga, having a podcast, astronomy, professional gamer, dance, director, computer programmer, environmentalist, and comedian.

"Wow, what a list. You are all sure to fail your way to changing the world!" proclaimed Mr. Ocean.

The class laughed.

"As much as we want to hear some examples of you telling Mom or Dad what you failed at in school, let's save that until the end of the day. Right now we have this week's OWWW quote to get to. Are you ready?"

"OWWW!" shouted the class.

"Drumroll please."

The students started tapping on their desks while Mr. Ocean peeled away the covered OWWW to reveal this week's quote.

An attitude of gratitude is the key to joy in your life.

"An attitude of gratitude is the key to joy in your life. Say it with me now, all together, class," said Mr. Ocean.

"An attitude of gratitude is the key to joy in your life," said the class.

"Yes, it most certainly is. And why is that? Why is this so important to your overall happiness and state of mind?"

A few hands went up.

"Yes, Aiden."

"I think it's because you have to appreciate what you have. I mean, things could most likely be better or they could be worse. You just have to be grateful for whatever it is you have," said Aiden.

"Very good point, Aiden. If you're not grateful for what you have, do you think that would change just by having a little more? What's interesting about this is that throughout my travels, I've been fortunate to meet people around the world, some of which were very wealthy, and some of which were extremely poor, monetarily speaking. Do you know what I found?"

The class was silent.

"What I found was that some of the happiest and most delightful people I've ever met were some of the poorest people I've come across. I'm talking about people living on perhaps just a few dollars a day. I once met a very poor woman that seemed to glow with happiness, and I asked her what her secret was. I'll never forget what she said. She said, 'I'm grateful for my life, and all that I have. I wish the best for everyone and have found that doing this is also good for me. As you radiate love, peace, and goodwill to all, you are really building a superstructure of happiness for all the days of your life.' Class, that was one of the wisest and most powerful things I have ever heard. It was a gift given to me freely and has stayed with me to this day."

"What I also found was that some of the wealthiest people I've met were also some of the most miserable and unhappy people I've known. Having a lot of money alone will not bring fulfillment. Yes, money can buy us nice things, but it's not the nice things that bring us how we want to feel inside ourselves, it's *gratitude* and appreciation that bring us joy," said Mr. Ocean.

"Would someone else like to make a comment on our quote?"

A few hands went up.

Yes, Marcela."

"Well, to go along with what you and Aiden said, I think it's good to want more for yourself and others, but I don't think having things different or having more is going to make someone happier. Whenever someone complains about wanting more, my uncle likes to remind us that the grass is not always greener on the other side," said Marcela.

"Excellent point, Marcela. I agree that we should strive for and pursue what we want in life, but while doing so, we need to see what's right in front of us and be grateful for what we already have. Happiness and joy are part of the journey, not the destination."

He waited for a few seconds before continuing.

"And to your uncle's point, the grass is not always greener on the other side. There's a very good chance that having something different or more will not bring someone any more joy, but it may very well leave someone unsatisfied. Always wanting more without being satisfied or grateful for what you have—does that sound like something you want for yourselves?"

"No," said the class.

"No, to achieve success without fulfillment is not actual success, nor is it the goal. To have both success and fulfillment, what do we need to do or focus on?" asked Mr. Ocean.

A few hands went up.

"Yes, Tony."

"From what we've talked about in here, we know that whatever we focus on expands. And that where your attention goes, your energy flows. Which means that the more you focus on what you have and what you're grateful for, the more you bring that into your life," said Tony.

"Outstanding answer, Tony. Energy flows where attention goes, and when you are genuinely grateful, it's something you can feel, which leads to inviting more of what you want to attract into your life. This aligns with a previous quote we introduced, when we talked about energy, frequency, and vibration. It's as if you are letting the universe know you are appreciative of what you've been given and welcome even more into your life to be grateful for. And the opposite is also true, isn't it? If we focus on the negative, we also bring more of that into our lives."

He paused for a moment.

"Who has a comment about gratitude when it comes to meditation?" asked Mr. Ocean.

A few students raised their hands.

"Yes, Liliana."

"I'm glad you asked about this because it's one of my favorite parts of our meditation. I love when you have us focus on things we're grateful for and the way it makes us feel. When we do this, I really feel gratitude for the things in my life. Also, when you have us focus on feeling the love from someone we're close to, it feels real," said Liliana.

"And how does this feeling of gratitude for what you have and the feeling of accepting someone's love make you feel?" asked Mr. Ocean.

"It makes me feel really good. It's something I look forward to every time we meditate and it's a good reminder for me to be grateful throughout the day," said Liliana.

"So, it's fair to say that feeling gratitude brings you joy?"

"Yes. And it's helped me gain a new perspective on feeling gratitude."

"Fantastic, Liliana, thank you for sharing. To take that a step further, class, gratitude can affect something you want to see happen or manifest in your life, which goes along with the use of visualization," said Mr. Ocean.

"Think about it—gratitude is being thankful for something that's already happened, and with gratitude you put yourself in a state of receiving. Gratitude is something you feel, so, when you visualize something you want, when you're grateful for it and feel like it's already happened, you open yourself up to receive this future something."

"This also goes along with what we've talked about before with acting, feeling, and thinking as if something's already happened.

Now, just add gratitude to that and you are setting yourself up for manifesting what you want. Pretty amazing, isn't it?"

"That's awesome, Mr. O!" exclaimed Aaron.

Mr. Ocean smiled, and then turned towards the whiteboard and started writing. When he was finished, he turned back and faced the class.

"Go ahead and write down this week's quote in your journal. And what I want you to add underneath the quote is what I just wrote on the board. Go ahead and say it with me before you write it," he directed.

"The magic word in life is attitude. Our attitude toward life determines life's attitude towards us," said the class.

What are your thoughts and most important takeaways from the chapter?

Are you living your life with an attitude of gratitude, and attracting more of what you want into your life, or do you need to make a shift in your mindset and attitude?

Chapter 26:

Practice and Share
[Auditorium]

"Speaking of adventures, do you remember me mentioning this at the beginning of our talk? I said this was an assembly for kids, by kids, and to think of this as a great adventure. Did you learn a lot and have a great adventure?" asked Viv.

Cheers could be heard throughout the audience, along with many students saying "yes," and someone shouting "no."

"Did I hear someone say no?" asked Viv.

"Show yourself!" exclaimed Leon.

The audience laughed.

"He's just kidding. Right, Leon?" asked Viv.

"Of course. You can never please everyone and that shouldn't be your goal, but it sounds like most of you enjoyed our talk and got something out of the assembly, which was our intention," said Leon.

"Thank you, Viv, thank you, Leon. And thank you for being such a gracious audience. The three of us have devoted our time and energy for your benefit without asking anything in return," said Mick.

"Wait—is this where we ask for something in return?" asked Viv.

"Yes," said Mick.

"I *knew* we were going to make some money on this!" said Viv.

"I don't think that's what he has in mind," said Leon.

"I know, I know, I'm joking ... kind of," said Viv.

Mick smiled and turned to face the audience again before speaking.

"You are now more knowledgeable and better equipped at making decisions for yourself than when you got out of bed this morning. What we ask of you in return for the knowledge you've gained are two things. The first is that you take it upon yourself to really make an effort to spend some quiet time alone by yourself each day. Doing so will reap many rewards. It will help you to connect to your inner wisdom and assist you along your path. It will help bring about what you want to see in your life. It will also start to change your reality and the way you view yourself, others, and the world around you," said Mick.

"And this quiet time can come in the form of meditation, mindfulness, and visualization," said Viv.

"Yeah, this is powerful stuff. This is wisdom you can use in the real world. And even though it might seem like a tall task to sit quietly every day, it's not if you start out doing it for just a little bit," said Leon.

"Very true. To make meditation part of your routine, make it as simple as you'd like. Take a few minutes in the morning, giving yourself the gift of no distractions, just focusing on your breathing. When your mind starts to wander come back to your breathing without judgment. That's it. By doing just that, you've learned how to meditate," said Mick.

"And the more often you do it, the better you'll get," said Viv.

"Yes. When you get comfortable meditating on your own, you can prolong it and start to add in mindfulness and visualization. You can add mindfulness to your meditation simply by being mindful of your breath, body and thoughts. You can also use visualization in the morning or in the evening before you go to bed," said Mick.

"And you mentioned earlier that mindfulness, another name for awareness, isn't just when we meditate; we can use it throughout the day, right?" asked Leon.

"Yes. As we discussed, you're capable of being mindful of your thoughts, beliefs, attitude, feelings, actions, and respond in a way that shows emotional intelligence. Meditating in the morning for just a few minutes will help your day unfold as you want it to, with intention, with the ability to respond to the day's events rather than react to them," said Mick.

"So, we're asking our audience to do two things. The first is to spend some quiet time alone each day. What's the second thing?" asked Viv.

"The second thing is to share what you've learned here with someone else. Many people don't know about the things we talked about today. Regardless of how young or old someone might be, sharing this information could change the perspective and feelings someone has about themselves, others and the world around them," said Mick.

"You can share the information you've learned today by talking about it. You can also share the information by checking out our website, wisdombeyondtheclassroom.com," said Leon.

"You were right about what we get in return, Mick. Sharing this information and what it can do for everyone here, including others, our communities, and our planet, is a far better exchange than us getting paid. Besides, we got out of school to be here today," said Viv.

Mick turned to face the principal, who gave Mick a smile and pointed to her wristwatch as if to say, "time is up."

Mick smiled back at the principal, faced Leon, and quietly said, "time."

"We've reached the end of our time and hope you got a lot out of what we talked about today. What we shared with you about how to meditate incorporates the essential parts of it, but there are many types of meditation. If you want to spend some time researching the different ways to meditate, we encourage that. From one visitor on this planet to another, thank you for letting us be visitors at your school today. I had a blast and hope you did too," said Leon smiling.

The audience cheered and someone yelled, "thank you."

"It should feel good to know that you're 1 in 400 trillion, and that if you expand your comfort zone, the universe will support you. And you just learned how to meditate like a boss. Like we talked about, if you incorporate meditation, mindfulness, and visualization into your life and make it part of your routine, you will empower yourself, follow your own path with intention, and bring out your superpowers. Thank you for being such a great audience!" said Viv enthusiastically.

Again, the audience cheered.

"You, me, and everyone on our planet is connected. This is more apparent now than it's ever been. We are each a spoke on the wheel of life. Although we may seem like we are separated because of dividing lines, borders, the color of our skin, how much money our families make, differing opinions, beliefs, and points of view, we are all brothers and sisters. That means the more you do for the greater good, by giving, loving, and serving, the more you will receive, and the more fulfilling your life will be. Thank you for being here and sharing your time with us today," said Mick.

As the audience started to cheer, the principal walked toward the three students and shook their hands.

"That was outstanding and really valuable. Thank you so much for your time. I'm so impressed with you three, and would love to have you back sometime," said the principal.

Turning to the audience, the principal said, "Lincoln High, what we learned here today was very valuable and something we can use in our lives every day. How about another round of applause for Viv, Mick, and Leon!"

The audience clapped and cheered loudly and rose to their feet to give a standing ovation. As the clapping and cheering faded, Mick, Leon, and Viv each took a step forward toward the audience.

"While you are standing, let's finish by doing something to connect one last time. Press your hands together with your fingertips touching and facing up. Place them at the center of your chest. Together we're going to close our eyes, bow and say 'namaste' to you, and you're going to do the same, repeating it back to us," said Mick.

"*Na*, like saying not without the t on the end of it, *ma*, like the first syllable in the word model, and *ste*, like stay cool. *Na-ma-ste*. Are you ready?" asked Leon.

The three friends paused for a moment and placed their hands in the center of their chest. They closed their eyes, bowed toward the audience, and said, "Namaste."

"Namaste," said the audience as they bowed back to Leon, Viv, and Mick.

What are your thoughts and most important takeaways from the chapter?

Where is the right place for you to start practicing what you've learned, when is a good time to start, and who will you share this information with?

Chapter 27:

Be Kind
[Classroom]

The following Wednesday when the students arrived at school, they were surprised to learn that they had a substitute teacher for the day.

"Do you know where Mr. Ocean is and when he'll be back? We have OWWW time today and a new quote to reveal!" exclaimed Jocelyn.

"I don't know about all that, but Mr. Ocean did leave me a letter," said Mrs. Baxter.

She read the letter silently to herself. It read:

Good morning Mrs. Baxter,

Thank you so much for stepping in as the teacher for today. Your job is an important one, and before your eyes are some of the brightest, most amazing students in the world.

Within this letter is an outline for you to follow, so that your day will go as smoothly as possible. I've also written a note to the students below. Please read it out loud. Thank you so much for all that you do. Have a wonderful day.

The students looked around eagerly, wondering what she was reading.

"Okay, class, here's a note from your teacher," said Mrs. Baxter.

She cleared her throat and began to read. This is what it said.

Dear Class,

I'm so sorry I can't be there today. I wish I could, but something came up that needs my attention. It may be a few days, but I will get back as soon as I can. I have not missed a day with you all year, so it feels a little strange to be writing you this letter, but it does remind me of something ... in the grand scheme of things, or in the big picture of life as they say, our time together is short. Although that's true, what you're learning this year can last you a lifetime. No matter our distance, or how much time will have passed since we last spoke or saw one another, if the wisdom you've gained stays with you and is a part of your life, I will always be close by.

Here's our OWWW quote for the week:

Be Kind

Our classroom quote today, "Be Kind," is simple yet impactful, and something you can do every single day. It's so important, that I've included an additional quote about kindness that I want you to remember and write down in your journal with this week's quote. The quote comes from the writer, Mark Twain. He said, "Kindness is the language which the deaf can hear and the blind can see."

You've learned enough to know that it's of the utmost importance to be loving and kind to yourself every day. Along with that, showing kindness to someone is one of the greatest gifts you can give, and it doesn't cost a thing. Being kind comes in many forms, usually in the words we speak and the actions we take. This can be done by offering a smile, writing a note, giving a compliment, doing an act of service, or just being warm and friendly. As emotional beings, it's in our nature to want to be recognized and feel appreciated. You have no idea what may be going on in someone's life or how they may be feeling inside. A simple act of kindness can turn someone's entire day around.

Your assignment that goes along with this week's quote asks two things of you. The first is to make sure you are treating yourself with kindness every day, and the second is to go out of your way to be kind to someone every day for the next week. As we've said before, the secret to living is giving. By giving without expecting anything in return, not only will you bring joy to others by showing kindness, studies have shown that doing so will increase your own happiness as well. So, give yourself permission to be as kind as you can to yourself and others, and take enjoyment in it. You will find that to "be kind" is one of the best habits you can form.

All my best,

Mr. Ocean

What are your thoughts and most important takeaways from the chapter?

Have you made it a habit yet to treat yourself with kindness and go out of your way to be kind to others? If not, now is a great time to start. What are some of your favorite lessons and quotes you learned throughout the book, and what are you going to do with the new "Wisdom Beyond the Classroom" you've gained?

Quote References

The primary cause of unhappiness is never the situation, but thoughts about it. Be aware of the thoughts you are thinking.
— *Eckhart Tolle*

You get in life what you have the courage to ask for.
— *Oprah Winfrey*

Faith is taking the first step, even when you don't see the whole staircase.
— *Martin Luther King, Jr.*

There was never a winner that wasn't a beginner.
— *Denis Waitley*

The ability to observe without evaluating is the highest form of intelligence.
— *Jiddu Krishnamurti*

You are a direct result of the thoughts you think, the people you spend time with, and the books you read.
— *Unknown*

The person who fails to plan, plans to fail.
— *Benjamin Franklin*

Desire backed by faith knows no such word as impossible.
— *Napoleon Hill*

The secret to living is giving.
— *Tony Robbins*

We make a living by what we get, but we make a life by what we give.
— *Winston Churchill*

Remember, your mind is your greatest asset, so be careful what you put into it.
— *Robert Kiyosaki*

Be the change you wish to see in the world.
— *Mahatma Gandhi*

The greatest secret is that you become what you think about.
— *Earl Nightingale*

Whether you like it or not, you create your life. Your dominant thoughts shape your life.
— *Vishen Lakhiani*

Everyone is a genius, but if you judge a fish by its ability to climb a tree, it will live its whole life believing that it is stupid.
— *Albert Einstein*

Spend time contemplating who you want to be. The mere process of contemplating who you want to be, begins to change your brain.
— *Joe Dispenza*

Everything is energy and that's all there is to it. Match the frequency of the reality you want, and you cannot help but get that reality. It can be no other way. This is not philosophy. This is physics.
— *Albert Einstein*

If you want to find the secrets of the universe, think in terms of energy, frequency, and vibration.
— *Nikola Tesla*

Whatever the mind can conceive and believe, it can achieve.
— *Napoleon Hill*

Yesterday's history, tomorrow's a mystery, today is a gift, and that's why it is called the present.
— *Alice Morse Earle*

If you're interested, you will do what is convenient; if you're committed, you'll do whatever it takes.
— *John Assaraf*

You can change your world by changing your words.
— *Joel Osteen*

Everything is created twice, first in your mind and then in reality.
— *Robin Sharma*

Your outer world is a reflection of your inner world.
— *T. Harv Eker*

In the midst of movement and chaos, keep stillness inside you.
— *Deepak Chopra*

Our lives are most affected by the way we think things are, not the way they are.
— Jim Rohn

If every eight-year-old in the world is taught meditation, we will eliminate violence from the world within one generation.
— the 14th Dalai Lama

We can never obtain peace in the outer world until we make peace within ourselves.
— the 14th Dalai Lama

Act as if you were already the person you most want to be.
— Brian Tracy

Live life as if everything is rigged in your favor.
— Rumi

Energy flows where attention goes.
— Michael Beckwith

Every time you are tempted to react in the same old way, ask if you want to be a prisoner of the past or a pioneer of the future.
— Deepak Chopra

It's been said that life is 10% of what happens to me and 90% of how I react to it.
— John Maxwell

If you want the subconscious to work for you, give it the right requests and attain its cooperation. It is always working for you.
— Joseph Murphy

A success mentality teaches not to waste energy on things that you can't change.
– Dean Graziosi

Hang out with people that make you stand on your tippy toes.
— Lisa Nichols

Watch your thoughts, they become your words, watch your words, they become your actions, watch your actions, they become your habits, watch your habits, they become your character, watch your character, it becomes your destiny.
– Lao Tzu

Make sure your habits are taking you where you want to go.
– Tom Bilyeu

Failure is part of success.
– Hank Aaron

The first thing successful people do is view failure as a positive signal to success.
— Brendon Burchard

I have not failed. I've just found 10,000 ways that won't work.
– Thomas Edison

Genius is 1% inspiration and 99% perspiration.
— Thomas Edison

In a growth mindset, challenges are exciting rather than threatening. So rather than thinking, oh, I'm going to reveal my weaknesses, you say, wow, here's a chance to grow.
— Carol Dweck

Stop letting people who do so little for you control so much of your mind, feelings, and emotions.
— *Will Smith*

Life is either a daring adventure or nothing at all.
— *Helen Keller*

As you radiate love, peace, and goodwill to all, you are really building a superstructure of happiness for all the days of your life.
– *Joseph Murphy*

Our attitude toward life determines life's attitude towards us.
– *Earl Nightingale*

Kindness is the language which the deaf can hear and the blind can see.
— *Mark Twain*

About the Author

Ryan Lockee is an avid learner and meditator, with great interest in the happiness, fulfillment, health, and development of us as individuals and as a society. He believes that with the right mindset, anything is possible.

Ryan has served as a high school baseball coach, a 4th and 6th grade teacher in San Francisco, California, and taught English in Seoul, South Korea. Ryan grew up as the oldest of six kids in Omaha, Nebraska, and currently lives with his wife and newborn son in San Francisco, California.

Ryan welcomes questions, comments, and conversation at www.wisdombeyondtheclassroom.com and would greatly appreciate it if you left a review on Amazon.